Frank Anstey

The travelling companions

A story in scenes

Frank Anstey

The travelling companions
A story in scenes

ISBN/EAN: 9783337242114

Printed in Europe, USA, Canada, Australia, Japan

Cover: Foto ©Andreas Hilbeck / pixelio.de

More available books at **www.hansebooks.com**

THE
TRAVELLING COMPANIONS

A Story in Scenes

[*Reprinted from "Punch"*]

BY

F. ANSTEY,

AUTHOR OF "VICE VERSÂ," "VOCES POPULI," ETC. ETC.

WITH TWENTY-SIX ILLUSTRATIONS
BY J. BERNARD PARTRIDGE

LONDON
LONGMANS, GREEN, AND CO.
AND NEW YORK: 15 EAST 16th STREET
1892

[*All rights reserved*]

CONTENTS

EXTREMES MEET
PODBURY PICKS UP ACQUAINTANCES
CULCHARD COMES OUT OF HIS SHELL
PODBURY IS UNPLEASANTLY SURPRISED
CULCHARD HAS THE BEST OF IT
CULCHARD MAKES A LITTLE MISCALCULATION
A DISSOLUTION OF PARTNERSHIP
PODBURY FINDS CONSOLATION
CULCHARD IS RATHER TOO CLEVER
PODBURY INSISTS ON AN EXPLANATION
COURTSHIP ACCORDING TO MR. RUSKIN
CULCHARD DESCENDS FROM THE CLOUDS
ON REVIENT TOUJOURS
MISS BANQUO
CULCHARD COMES OUT NOBLY
CULCHARD FEELS SLIGHTLY UNCOMFORTABLE
CULCHARD CANNOT BE "HAPPY WITH EITHER"
A SUSPENSION OF HOSTILITIES
CRUMPLED ROSELEAVES
PUT NOT YOUR FAITH IN FIDIBUS
WEARING RUE WITH A DIFFERENCE
ONE MAN'S MEAT; ANOTHER MAN'S POISON
PEARLS AND PIGS
THE PILGRIMS OF LOVE
JOURNEYS END IN LOVERS' MEETING
PODBURY KISSES THE ROD

ILLUSTRATIONS

	PAGE
"YES, SIR"	3
"WANTED TO KNOW IF YOU WERE MY TUTOR"	11
"LEESTEN, I DELL YOU VONCE MORE"	17
"I PRESUME, THOUGH, HE SLEPT BAD, NIGHTS"	22
MR. CYRUS K. TROTTER DISCUSSING NEW YORK HOTELS	26
"GOOD HEAVENS, IT—IT'S GONE!"	33
"PUTS ME IN MIND O' THE BEST PART O' BOX 'ILL"	39
"ER—I HAVE BROUGHT YOU THE PHILOSOPHICAL WORK I MENTIONED"	46
PODBURY GRAPPLING WITH THE EPITOME OF SPENCER	50
THE CURATE GETS UP AND QUITS THE ROOM WITH DIGNITY	57
"IT DOES SEEM RATHER ROUGH ON FELLOWS, DON'T YOU KNOW"	63
AN ELDERLY ENGLISHWOMAN IS SITTING ON HER TRUNK	66
STRUGGLING WITH A LONG PRINTED PANORAMA	73
"HOW LITTLE YOU KNOW ME!"	79
"I KNOCK OFF QUITE A NUMBER OF THESE WHILE I'M ABROAD LIKE THIS"	84
"BOUND TO TEACH YOU A LOT, SEEING ALL THE OLD ALTAR-PIECES I DO!"	90
"I DON'T KNOW IF YOU'RE ACQUAINTED WITH A PAPER CALLED THE 'PENNY PATRICIAN'?"	95
SHE PASSES ON WITH HER CHIN IN THE AIR!	101
"BELLISSIMO SCULTORE!"	107
"HI! OTEZ-MOI CECI!"	113
"I GUESS YOU WANT TO COLOGNE *your* CHEEKS—THEY'RE DREADFUL LUMPY"	120
"I GUESS YOU'RE THE MOST UNSELFISH SAINT ON TWO LEGS!"	127
A SOLEMN GENTLEMAN STRUGGLING WITH A TROUBLESOME COUGH	132
"A MEAN CUSS? ME! REALLY—!"	137
HYPATIA, BY JOVE! NARROW SHAVE THAT!	143
READS WITH A GRADUALLY LENGTHENING COUNTENANCE	150

THE
TRAVELLING COMPANIONS

CHAPTER I.

Extremes Meet.

SCENE—*An Excursion Agent's Offices. Behind the counters polite and patient Clerks are besieged by a crowd of Intending Tourists, all asking questions at once.*

FIRST INTENDING TOURIST. Here—have you made out that estimate for me yet?

CLERK. In one moment, Sir. (*He refers to a list, turns over innumerable books, jots down columns of francs, marks, and florins; reduces them to English money, and adds them up.*) First class fares on the Rhine, Danube and Black Sea steamers, I think you said, second class rail, and postwagen?

FIRST INT. T. I did say so, I believe; but you had better make it second class all through, and I can always pay the difference if I want to.

[*The* CLERK *alters the sums accordingly, and adds up again.*

CLERK. Fifty-five pounds fourteen and a penny, Sir. Shall I make you out the tickets now?

FIRST INT. T. Um, no. On second thoughts, I'd like to see one of your short Circular Tours for the English Lakes, or Wales, before I decide.

[*The* CLERK *hands him a quantity of leaflets, with which he retires.*

Enter MR. CLARENDON CULCHARD, *age about twenty-eight; in Somerset House; tall; wears glasses, stoops slightly, dresses carefully, though his tall hat is of the last fashion but two. He looks about him expectantly, and then sits down to wait.*

CULCHARD (*to himself*). No sign of him yet! I *do* like a man to keep an appointment. If this is the way he *begins*—I have my doubts whether he is *quite* the sort of fellow to—but I took the precaution to ask Hugh Rose about him, and Rose said he was the best company in the world, and I couldn't help getting on with him. I don't think Rose would deceive me. And from all I've seen of Podbury, he seems a pleasant fellow enough. What a Babel! All these people bent on pleasure, going to seek it in as many directions—with what success no one can predict. There's an idea for a sonnet there.

[*He brings out a pocket-book, and begins to write*—"As when a——"

AN AMURRCAN CITIZEN (*to* CLERK). See here, I've been around with your tickets in Yurrup, and when I was at Vernis, I bought some goods at a store there, and paid cash down for 'em, and they promised to send 'em on for me right here, and that was last fall, and I've never heard any more of 'em, and what I want *you* should do now is to instruct your representative at Vernis to go round and hev a talk with that man, and ask him what in thunder he means by it, and kinder hint that he'll hev the Amurrean Consul in his hair pretty smart, if he don't look slippier!

[*The* CLERK *mildly suggests that it would be better to communicate directly with the American Consulate, or with the tradesman himself.*

THE A. C. But hold on—how 'm I goin' to write to that sharp, when I've lost his address, and disremember his name? Can't you mail a few particulars to your agent, so he'll identify him? No? (*Disappointed.*) Well, I thought you'd ha' fixed up a little thing like that, anyhow; in my country they'd ha' done it right away. Yes, *Sir!*

[*He goes away in grieved surprise.*

Extremes Meet. 3

Enter MR. JAMES PODBURY, *age twenty-six; in a City Office; short, fresh-coloured, jaunty; close-cut dark hair. Not having been to the City to-day, he is wearing light tweeds, and brown boots.*

PODBURY (*to himself*). Just nicked it!—(*looks at clock*)—more or less.

And he doesn't seem to have turned up yet. Wonder how we shall hit it off together. Hughie Rose said he was a capital good chap—when you once got over his manner. Anyhow, it's a great tip to go abroad with a fellow who knows the ropes. (*Suddenly sees* CULCHARD *absorbed in his note-book.*) So *here* you are, eh?

CULCH. (*slightly scandalized by the tweeds and the brown boots*). Yes, I've been here some little time. I wish you could have managed to come before, because they close early here to-day, and I wanted to go thoroughly over the tour I sketched out before getting the tickets.

[*He produces an elaborate outline.*

PODB. (*easily*). Oh, *that's* all right! I don't care where *I* go! All I want is, to see as much as we can in the time—leave all the rest to you. I'll sit here while you get the tickets.

AN OLD LADY (*to* CLERK, *as* CULCHARD *is waiting at the counter*). Oh, I *beg* your pardon, but *could* you inform me if the 1·55 train from Calais to Basle stops long enough for refreshments anywhere, and where they examine the luggage, and if I can leave my hand-bag in the carriage, and whether there is an English service at Yodeldorf, and is it held in the hotel, and Evangelical, or High Church, and are the sittings free, and what Hymn-book they use?

[*The* CLERK *sets her mind free on as many of these points as he can, and then attends to* CULCHARD.

CULCH. (*returning to* PODBURY *with two cases bulging with books of coloured coupons*). Here are yours. I should like you to run your eye over them, and see that they are correct, if you don't mind.

PODB. (*stuffing them in his pocket*). Can't be bothered now. Take your word for it.

CULCH. No—but considering that we start the first thing to-morrow morning, wouldn't it be as well to have some idea of where you're going? And, by the way, excuse me, but is it altogether prudent to keep your tickets in an outside pocket like that? I always keep mine, with my money, in a special case in an inner pocket, with a buttoned flap—then I know I *can't* lose them.

PODB. Anything for a quiet life! (*He examines his coupons.*) Dover to Ostend? Never been there—like to see what Ostend's like. But why didn't you go by Calais?—*shorter*, you know.

CULCH. Because I thought we'd see Bruges and Ghent on our way to Brussels.

PODB. Bruges, eh? Capital! Anything particular going on there? No? It don't matter. And Ghent—let's see, wasn't that where they brought the good news from? Yes, we'll stop at Ghent—if we've time. Then—Brussels? Good deal of work to be done there, I suppose, sightseeing, and that? I like a place where you can moon about without being bothered myself; now, at *Brussels*—never mind, I was only thinking.

CULCH. It's the best place to get to Cologne and up the Rhine from. Then, you see, we go rather out of our way to Nuremberg——

PODB. Where they make toys? *I* know—pretty festive there, eh?

CULCH. I don't know about festive—but it is—er—a quaint, and highly interesting old place. Then I thought we'd dip down to Constance, and strike across the Alps to the Italian Lakes.

PODB. Italian Lakes? First-rate! Yes, *they*'re worth seeing, I suppose. Think they're better than the *Swiss* ones, though?

CULCH. (*tolerantly*). I can get the coupons changed for Switzerland if you prefer it. The Swiss Lakes may be the more picturesque.

PODB. Yes, we'll do Switzerland—and run back by Paris, eh? Not much to do in Switzerland, though, after all!

CULCH. (*with a faintly superior smile*). There are one or two mountains, I believe. But, personally, I should prefer Italy.

PODB. So should I. No fun in mountains—unless you go up 'em. What do you think of choosing some quiet place, where nobody ever goes —say in France or Germany—and, sticking to *that*. More of a rest, wouldn't it be? such a bore having to know a lot of people!

CULCH. I don't see how we can change *all* the tickets, really. If you like, we could stop a week at St. Goarshausen.

PODB. What's St. Goarshausen like—cheery?

CULCH. I understood the idea was to keep away from our fellow countrymen, and as far as I can remember St. Goarshausen, it is not overrun with tourists—we should be quiet enough *there*.

PODB. That's the place for *me*, then. Or could we push on to Vienna? Never seen Vienna.

CULCH. If you like to give up Italy altogether.

PODB. What do you say to *beginning* with Italy and working back? Too hot, eh? Well, then, we'll let things be as they are—I dare say it will do well enough. So *that's* settled!

CULCH. (*to himself on parting, after final arrangements concluded*). I wish Rose had warned me that Podbury's habit of mind was so painfully desultory. (*He sighs.*) However——

PODB. (*to himself*). Wonder how long I shall take to get over Culchard's manner. (*He sighs.*) I wish old Hughie was coming—he'd give me a leg over! [*He walks on thoughtfully.*

CHAPTER II.

Podbury picks up Acquaintances.

SCENE—*Courtyard of the "Grand Hôtel du Lion Belgique et d'Albion," at Brussels. It is just after table d'hôte;* PODBURY *and* CULCHARD *are sitting on a covered terrace, with coffee.*

PODBURY (*producing a pipe*). Not such a bad dinner! Expect they'll rook us a lot for it, though. Rather fun, seeing the waiters all troop in with a fresh course, when the proprietor rang his bell. Like a ballet at the Empire—eh?

CULCHARD (*selecting a cigarette*). I'm not in a position to say. I don't affect those places of entertainment myself.

PODB. Oh! Where *do* you turn in when you want to kick up your heels a bit? Madame Tussaud's? I say, why on earth didn't you talk to that old Johnny next to you at dinner? He was trying all he knew to be friendly.

CULCH. Was he? I dare say. But I rather understood we came out with the idea of keeping out of all that.

PODB. Of course. *I'm* not keen about getting to know people. He had no end of a pretty daughter, though. Mean to say you didn't spot her?

CULCH. If by "spotting" you mean—was I aware of the existence of a very exuberant young person, with a most distressing American accent?—I can only say that she made her presence sufficiently evident. I confess she did not interest me to the point of speculating upon her relationship to anybody else.

PODB. Well—if you come to that, I don't know that I—still, she was uncommonly—— (*Happens to glance round, and lowers his voice.*) Jove! she's in the Reading-room, just behind us. (*Hums, with elaborate carelessness.*) La di deedle-lumpty—loodle-oodle-loo——

CULCH. *who detests humming*. By the way, I wish you hadn't been in such a hurry to come straight on. I particularly wished to stop at Bruges, and see the Memlings.

PODB. I do like that! For a fellow who means to keep out of people's way! They'd have wanted you to stay to lunch and dinner, most likely.

CULCH. *roused to epigram*. Hardly, my dear fellow—they're pictures, as it happens.

PODB. *unabashed*. Oh, are they? Any way, you've fetched up your average here. Weren't there enough in the Museum for you?

CULCH. *piqued*. You surely wouldn't call the collection here exactly representative of the best period of Flemish Art?

PODB. If you ask me, I should call it a simply footling show—but you were long enough over it. CULCHARD *shudders slightly, and presently sets his profile*. What's up now? Nothing gone wrong with the works, eh?

CULCH. *with dignity*. No—I was merely feeling for my note-book. I had a sudden idea for a sonnet, that's all.

PODB. Ah, you shouldn't have touched those mussels they gave us with the sole. Have a nip of this cognac, and you'll soon be all right.

(CULCHARD *is—here he is too late aware*—PODBURY *by* MR. CYRUS K. TROTTER *and by his wife*, MAID S. TROTTER. *They are by this glared down out of the Salle de Lecture and have to continue their conversation outside.*)

Miss TROTTER. Well, I guess it's gayer out here, anyway. That Reading-room is 'bout as cheerful as a burying lot with all the tombs open. I never thought much of that man who said that Brussels was a small Paris.

MR. TROTTER. Maybe we aren't been long enough off the cars to judge yet. Do you feel like putting on your hat and sack and setter

Podbury picks up Acquaintances.

MISS T. Not any. I expect the old city will have to curb its impatience to see me till to-morrow. I'm tired some.

CULCH. *(to himself)*. Confound it, how can I——! *(Looks up, and observes* MISS T. *with a sudden attention.)* That fellow Podbury has better taste than I gave him credit for. She *is* pretty—in her peculiar style—*quite* pretty! Pity she speaks with that deplorable accent.

[*Writes*—"*Vermilion lips that sheathe a parrot tongue,*" *and runs over all the possible rhymes to "tongue."*

PODB. *(observing that his pencil is idle)*. Gas cut off again? Come for a toddle. You don't mean to stick here all the evening, eh?

CULCH. Well, we might take a turn later on, and see the effect of St. Gudule in the moonlight.

PODB. Something *like* a rollick that! But what do you say to dropping in quietly at the Eden for an hour or so, eh? Variety show and all that going on.

CULCH. Thanks—variety shows are not much in my line; but don't mind me if you want to go.

[PODBURY *wanders off, leaving* CULCHARD *free to observe* MISS TROTTER.

MISS T. Charley writes he's having a lovely time in Germany going round. I guess he isn't feeling so cheap as he did. I wish he'd come along right here.

MR. T. I presume he's put in all the time he had for Belgium—likely we'll fetch up against him somewhere before he's through.

MISS T. Well, and I don't care how soon we do, either. Charley's a bright man, and real cultivated. I'm always telling him that he's purrfectly splendid company, considering he's only a cousin.

MR. T. That's so every time. I like Charley Van Boodeler firstrate myself.

CULCH. *(to himself)*. If Charley Van Boodeler was *engaged* to her, I suppose he'd be there. Pshaw! What *does* it matter? Somehow, I rather wish now that I'd—but perhaps we shall get into conversation presently. Hang it, here's that fellow Podbury back again! Wish to goodness he'd——'*To* PODBURY.' Hallo, so you haven't started yet?

PODB. Been having a talk with the porter. He says there's a big fair

c

over by the Station du Midi, and it's worth seeing. Are you game to come along and sample it, eh?

CULCH. (*with an easy indifference intended for* MISS T.'s *benefit*). No, I think not, thanks. I'm very comfortable where I am.

[*He resumes his writing.*

PODB. Well, it's poor fun having to go alone!

[*He is just going, when* MR. TROTTER *rises and comes towards him.*

MR. T. You'll excuse me, Sir, but did I overhear you remark that there was a festivity in progress in this city?

PODB. So I'm told; a fair, down in the new part. I could tell you how to get to it, if you thought of going.

MR. T. Well, I don't see how I should ever strike that fair for myself, and I guess if there's anything to be seen we're bound to *see* it, so me and my darter—allow me to introduce my darter to you—Maud, this gentleman is Mr.—I don't think I've caught your name, Sir—Podbury?—Mr. Podbury, who's kindly volunteered to conduct us round.

MISS T. *I* should have thought you'd want to leave the gentleman some say in the matter, father—not to mention me!

PODB. (*eagerly*). But won't you come? Do. I shall be awfully glad if you will!

MISS T. If it makes you so glad as all that, I believe I'll come. Though what you could say different, after Poppa had put it up so steep on you, *I* don't know. I'll just go and fix myself first. [*She goes.*

MR. T. (*to* PODBURY). My only darter, Sir, and a real good girl. We come over from the States, crossed a month ago to-day, and seen a heap already. Been runnin' all over Scotland and England, and kind of looked round Ireland and Wales, and now what *we've* got to do is to see as much as we can of Germany and Switzerland and It'ly, and get some idea of France before we start home this fall. I guess we're both of us gettin' pretty considerable homesick already. My darter was sayin' to me on'y this evening at *table d'hôte*, "Father," she sez, "the vurry first thing we'll do when we get home is to go and hev a good square meal of creamed oysters and clams with buckwheat cakes and maple syrup." Don't seem as if we *could* git along without maple syrup *much*

Podbury picks up Acquaintances. 11

longer. (MISS TROTTER *returns*.) You never mean going out without your gums?

MISS T. I guess it's not damp here--any. (*To* PODBURY.) Now

"WANTED TO KNOW IF YOU WERE MY TUTOR!" [*He roars.*

you're going to be *Mary*, and father and I have got to be the little lambs and follow you around.

[*They go out, leaving* CULCHARD *annoyed with himself and everybody else, and utterly unable to settle down to his sonnet again.*

IN AN UPPER CORRIDOR TWO HOURS LATER.

CULCH. (*coming upon* PODBURY). So you've got rid of your Americans at last, eh?

PODB. *I* was in no hurry, I can tell you. She's a ripping little girl —tremendous fun. What do you think she asked me about *you*?

CULCH. (*stiff, but flattered*). I wasn't aware she had honoured me by her notice. What *was* it?

PODB. Said you had a sort of schoolmaster look, and wanted to know if you were my tutor. My tutor! [*He roars.*

CULCH. I hope you—ah—undeceived her?

PODB. Rather! Told her it was t'other way round, and I was looking after *you*. Said you were suffering from melancholia, but were not absolutely dangerous.

CULCH. If that's your idea of a joke, all I can say is——

[*He chokes with rage.*

PODB. (*innocently*). Why, my dear chap, I thought you wanted 'em kept out of your way!

[CULCHARD *slams his bedroom door with temper, leaving* PODBURY *outside, still chuckling.*

CHAPTER III.

Culchard comes out of his Shell.

SCENE—*On the Coach from Braine l'Alleud to Waterloo. The vehicle has a Belgian driver, but the conductor is a true-born Briton.* MR. CYRUS K. TROTTER *and his daughter are behind with* PODBURY. CULCHARD, *who is not as yet sufficiently on speaking terms with his friend to ask for an introduction, is on the box-seat in front.*

MR. TROTTER. How are you getting along, Maud? Your seat pretty comfortable?

MISS TROTTER. Well, I guess it would be about as luxurious if it hadn't got a chunk of wood nailed down the middle—it's not going to have any one confusing it with a bed of roses *just* yet. (*To* PODB.) Your friend mad about anything? He don't seem to open his head more'n he's obliged to. I presume he don't approve of your taking up with me and father—he keeps away from us considerable, I notice.

PODB. (*awkwardly*). Oh—er—I wouldn't say that, but he's a queer kind of chap rather, takes prejudices into his head and all that. I wouldn't trouble about him if I were you—not worth it, y' know.

MISS T. Thanks—but it isn't going to shorten my existence any.

[CULCH. *overhears all this, with feelings that may be imagined.*

BELGIAN DRIVER (*to his horses*). Pullep! Allez vite! Bom-bom-bom! Alright!

CONDUCTOR (*to* CULCHARD). 'E's very proud of 'is English, 'e is. 'Ere, Jewls, ole feller, show the gen'lm'n 'ow yer can do a swear. (*Belgian Driver utters a string of English imprecations with the utmost fluency and good-nature.*) 'Ark at 'im now! Bust my frogs! (*Admiringly, and not without a sense of the appropriateness of the phrase.*) But he's a caution, Sir, ain't he? *I taught him most o' what he knows!*

A FRENCH PASSENGER (*to* CONDUCTOR). Dis donc, mon ami, est-ce qu'on peut voir d'ici le champ de bataille?

COND. (*with proper pride*). It ain't no use your torkin *to me*, Mossoo; I don't speak no French myself. (*To* CULCHARD.) See that field there, Sir?

CULCH. (*interested*). On the right? Yes; what happened *there?*

COND. Fine lot o' rabbits inside o' there—big fat 'uns. (*To another Passenger.*) No, Sir, that ain't Belly Lions as you see from 'ere; that's Mon Sin Jeean, and over there Oogymong, and Challyroy to the left.

ON THE TOP OF THE MOUND.

CULCHARD, *who has purchased a map in the Waterloo Museum as a means of approaching* MISS TROTTER, *is pounced upon by an elderly Belgian Guide in a blue blouse, from whom he finds it difficult to escape.*

THE GUIDE (*fixing* CULCHARD *with a pair of rheumy eyes and a gnarled forefinger*). You see vere is dat schmall voodt near de vite 'ouse? not dere, along my shdeck—so. Dat is vare Peeeton vas kill, Inglis Officer, Peeeton. Two days pefore he was voundet in de ahum. 'E say to his sairvan', "You dell ennipoddies, I keel you!" He vandt to pe in ze bataille: he *vas* in ze bataille—seven lance troo 'im, seven; Peeeton, Inglis Officer. (CULCHARD *nods his head miserably.*) Hah, you 'ave de shart dere—open 'im out vide, dat de odder shentilmans see. (CULCHARD *obeys, spell-bound.*) Vare you see dat blue gross, Vaterloo Shirshe, vere Loart Uxbreedge lose 'is laig. Zey cot 'im off and pury him in ze cottyardt, and a villow grow oudt of 'im. 'E com 'ere to see the villow growing oudt of his laig.

CULCH. (*abandoning his map, and edging towards* MISS TROTTER). Hem—we are gazing upon one of the landmarks of our national history—Miss Trotter.

MISS T. That's a vurry interesting re-mark. I presume you must

Culchard comes out of his Shell.

have studied up some for a reflection of that kind. Mr. Podbury, your friend has been telling me—— [*She repeats* CULCHARD'S *remark.*
PODB. (*with interest*). Got any *more* of those, old fellow?

[CULCHARD *moves away with disgusted hauteur.*

THE GUIDE (*re-capturing him*). Along dat gross vay, Vellainton meet Blushair. Prussian général, Blushair. Vellainton 'e com hier. I see 'im. Ven 'e see ze maundt, 'e vos vair angri. 'E say, "Eet is no ze battle-fiel' no more—I com back nevare!" Zat aidge is vere de Scots Greys vas. Ven they dell Napoleon 'oo zey are, 'e say, "Fine mens— splendid mens, I feenish dem in von hour!" Soult 'e say, "Ah, Sire, you do not know dose dairible grey 'orses!" Napoleon 'e *not* know dem. Soult 'e meet dem at de Peninsulaire—'e know dem. In dat Shirsh, dventy, dirty dablets to Inglis officers. Napoleon 'e coaled op 'is laift vink, zey deploy in line, vair you see my shdeek—ha, ze shentelman is gone avay vonce more!

MISS T. (*to* CULCHARD, *who has found himself unable to keep away*). You don't seem to find that old gentleman vurry good company?

CULCH. The fact is that I much prefer to receive my impressions of a scene like this in solitude.

MISS T. *I* should have thought you'd be too polite to tell me so; but I was moving on, anyway.

[*She goes on. Before* CULCHARD *can follow and explain, he finds himself accosted by* MR. TROTTER.

MR. T. I don't know as I'm as much struck by this Waterloo field as I expected, Sir. As an Amurrcan, I find it doesn't come up to some of our battlefields in the War. We don't blow about those battlefields, Sir, but for style and general picturesqueness, I ain't seen nothing *this* side to equal them. You ever been over? You want to come over and see our country—that's what *you* want to do. You mustn't mind me a-running on, but when I meet some one as I can converse with in my own language— well, I just about talk myself dry.

[*He talks himself dry, until rejoined by the* GUIDE *with* PODBURY *and* MISS TROTTER.

GUIDE (*to* PODBURY). Leesten, I dell you. My vader—eighteen, no in ze Airmi, laboreur man—he see Napoleon standt in a saircle; officers roundt 'im. Boots, op to hier; green cott; vite vaiscott; vite laigs——

Podb. Your father's legs?

Guide (*indignantly*). No, Sare; my vader see Napoleon's laigs; leedle 'at, qvite plain; no faither—nossing.

Podb. But you just said you *had* a faither!

Guide. I say, Napoleon 'ad no faither—vat you call it?—*plume*—in 'is 'at, at ze bataille.

Podb. Are you sure? I thought the history books said he "stuck a feather in his hat, and called it Macaroni."

Miss T. I presume you're thinking of our National Amurrcan character, Yankee Doodle?

Guide. My vader, 'e no see Napoleon viz a Yankedoodle in 'is 'at; 'e vear nossing.

Podb. Nothing? What became of the green coat and white waistcoat, then, eh?

Guide. Ah, you unnerstan' nossing at all! Leesten, I dell you vonce more. My vader——

Podb. No, look here, my friend; you go and tell *that* gentleman all about it (*indicating* Culchard); he's very interested in hearing what Napoleon wore or didn't wear.

[*The* Guide *takes possession of* Culchard *once more, who submits, under the impression that* Miss Trotter *is a fellow-sufferer.*

Guide (*concluding a vivid account of the fight at Houguymont*). Bot ven zey com qvite nearer, zey vind ze rade line no ze Inglis soldiers—nossing bot a breek vall, viz ze moskets—"Prown Pesses," you coal dem—shdeekin out of ze 'oles! Ze 'oles schdill dere. Dat vas Houguymont, in the orshairde. Now you com viz me and see ze lion. Ze dail, two piece; ze bodi, von piece; ze ball, von piece. I sank you, Sare. 'Ope you com again soon.

[Culchard *discovers that the* Trotters *and* Podbury *have gone down some time ago. At the foot of the steps he finds his friend waiting for him, alone.*

Culch. (*with stiff politeness*). Sorry you considered it necessary to

Culchard comes out of his Shell.

stay behind on my account. I see your American friends have already started for the station.

PODB. (*gloomily*). There were only two seats on that coach, and they

"LEESTEN, I DELL YOU VONCE MORE."

wouldn't wait for the next. I don't know why, unless it was that they saw *you* coming down the steps. She can't stand you at any price.

CULCH. (*with some heat*). Just as likely she had had enough of your buffoonery!

PODB. (*with provoking good humour*). Come, old chap, don't get your shirt out with *me*. Not my fault if she's found out you think yourself too big a swell for her, is it?

CULCH. (*hotly*). When did I say so—or think so? It's what you've told her about me, and I must say I call it——

Podb. Don't talk bosh! Who said she was forward and bad form and all the rest of it in the courtyard that first evening? She was close by, and heard every word of it, I shouldn't wonder.

Culch. (*colouring*). It's not of vital importance if she did. (*Whistling*.) Few-fee-fee-foo-foodle-di-fee-di-fa-foo.

Podb. Not a bit—to her. Better step out if we mean to catch that train. (*Humming.*) La-di-loodle-lumpty-leedle-um-ti-loo!

[*They step out,* Podbury *humming pleasantly and* Culchard *whistling viciously, without further conversation, until they arrive at Braine l'Alleud Station—and discover that they have just missed their train.*

CHAPTER IV.

Podbury is unpleasantly Surprised.

SCENE—*The Wiertz Museum at Brussels, a large and well-lighted gallery containing the works of the celebrated Belgian, which are reducing a limited number of spectators to the usual degree of stupefaction. Enter* CULCHARD, *who seats himself on a central ottoman.*

CULCH. (*to himself*). If Podbury won't come down to breakfast at a decent hour, he can't complain if I—— I wonder if he heard Miss Trotter say she was thinking of coming here this morning. Somehow, I *should* like that girl to have a more correct comprehension of my character. I don't so much mind her thinking me fastidious and exclusive. I dare say I *am*—but I *do* object to being made out a hopeless melancholiac! (*He looks round the walls.*) So these are Wiertz's masterpieces, eh? h'm. Strenuous, vigorous,—a trifle crude, perhaps. Didn't he refuse all offers for his pictures during his lifetime? Hardly think he could have been overwhelmed with applications for the one opposite. (*He regards an enormous canvas, representing a brawny and gigantic Achilles perforating a brown Trojan with a small mast.*) Not a dining-room picture. Still, I like his independence—work up rather well in a sonnet. Let me see. (*He takes out note-book and scribbles.*) "He scorned to ply his sombre brush for hire." Now if I read that to Podbury, he'd pretend to think I was treating of a shoe-black on strike! Podbury is so utterly deficient in reverence.

[*Close by is a party of three Tourists—a Father and Mother, and a Daughter; who is reading to them aloud from the somewhat effusive Official Catalogue; the education of all three appears to have been elementary.*

THE DAUGHTER (*spelling out the words laboriously*). "I could not 'elp fancying this was the artist's por-portrait?—portent?—no, *protest* against des-des—'*recklessly*, despoticism, and tyranny, but I see it is only—Por-Porlifiymus fasting upon the companions of Ulyces."

HER MALE PARENT. Do it tell yer what that there big arm and leg be a-doin' of in the middle of 'em?

DAUGHTER (*stolidly*). Don't you be in a nurry, father (*continuing*)— " in the midst of some colonial?—*That* ain't it—*colossial* animiles fanatic-ally—fan-tasty-cally——" why, this catalogue is 'alf foreign itself!

FEMALE P. Never mind, say 'Peterborough' at the 'ard words—*we* shan't be none the wiser!

DAUGHTER. "The sime-boalic ram the 'ero is to Peterborough and leave 'is Peterborough grotter——"

MALE P. That'll do—read what it says about the next one.

DAUGHTER (*reading*). "The Forge of Vulkin. Words are useless 'ere. Before sech a picture one can but look, and think, and enjoy it."

BOTH PARENTS (*impressed*). Lor!

[*They smack their lips reverently*; MISS TROTTER *enters the Gallery.*

CULCH. (*rising and going to meet her*). Good morning, Miss Trotter. We—ah—meet again.

MISS T. That's an undeniable fact. I've left Poppa outside. Poppa restricts himself to exteriors wherever he can—says he doesn't seem to mix up his impressions so much that way. But you're alone, too. Where 've you hitched your friend up?

CULCH. My friend did not rise sufficiently early to accompany me. And, by the way, Miss Trotter, I should like to take this opportunity of disabusing your mind of the—er—totally false impression——

MISS T. Oh, *that's* all right. I told him he needn't try to give me away, for I could see you weren't *that* kind of man!

CULCH. (*gratefully*). Your instinct was correct—perfectly correct. When you say "that kind of man," I presume you refer to the description my—er—friend considered it humorous to give of me as an unsociable hypochondriac?

MISS T. Well, no; he didn't say just that. He represented you as

Podbury is unpleasantly Surprised.

one of the fonniest persons alive ; said you told stories which tickled folks to death almost.

CULCII. (*annoyed*). Really, this is *most* unpardonable of Mr. Podbury! To have such odious calumnies circulated about one behind one's back is simply too——I do *not* aspire to—ah—to tickle folks to death!

MISS T. (*soothingly*). Well, I guess there's no harm done. I didn't feel like being in any imminent danger of perishing that way in your society. You're real high-toned and ever so improving, and that's better than tickling, every time. And I want you to show me round this collection and give me a few notions. Seems to me there was considerable sand in Wiertz ; sort of spread himself around a good deal, didn't he? I presume, though, he slept bad, nights. (*She makes the tour of the Gallery, accompanied by* CULCHARD, *who admires her, against his better judgment, more and more.*) . . . I declare if that isn't your friend Mr. Podbury just come in! I believe I'll have to give you up to him.

CULCII. (*eagerly*). I beg you will not think it necessary. He—he has a guide already. *He* does not require my services. And, to be plain, my poor friend—though an excellent fellow according to his—ah—lights—is a companion whose society occasionally amounts to a positive infliction.

MISS T. Well, I find him too chinny myself, times. Likely he won't notice us if we don't seem to be aware of him.

[*They continue to inspect the canvases.*

A BELGIAN GUIDE (*who has made an easy capture of* PODBURY *at the Hotel entrance*). Hier now is a shdrainch beecture. "De toughts and veesions of a saivered haid." Fairsst meenut afder degapitation ; de zagonde ; de tirt. Hier de haid tink dey vant to poot him in a goffin. Dere are *two* haids—von goes op, de udder down. Haf you got de two? Nod yet? No?

PODBURY (*shaking his head sagaciously*). Oh, ah, yes. Capital. Rum subject, though.

GUIDE. Yais, vary magnifique, vary grandt, and—and rom also! Dees von rebresents Napoleon in hail. De modders show him de laigs and ahums of dair sons keeled in de vars, and invide him to drink a cop of bloodt.

Pode. Ha, cheery picture that!
Guide. Cheery, oh, yais! Now com and beep troo dis 'ole. (Podbury

"I PRESUME, THOUGH, HE SLEPT BAD, NIGHTS."

obeys with docility.) You see? A Mad Voman cooking her shildt in a gettle. Hier again, dey haf puried a man viz de golera pefore he is daid, he dries to purst de gofiin, you see only de handt shdicking oudt.

Pode. The old Johnny seems full of pretty fancies. (*He looks through*

Podbury is unpleasantly Surprised. 23

another peephole.) Girl looking at skeleton. Ha! Any other domestic subjects on view? (*He suddenly sees* MISS TROTTER *and* CULCHARD *with their backs to him.*) Hal—lo, this *is* luck! I must go to the rescue, or that beggar Culchard will bore her to death in no time. (*To* GUIDE.) Here, hold on a minute. (*Crosses to* CULCHARD, *followed by* GUIDE.) How d' ye do, Miss Trotter? Doing the Wild Wiertz Show, I see. Ah, Culchard, why didn't you tell me you were going—might have gone together. I say, I've got a guide here.

CULCH. (*drily*). So we perceive—a very sensible plan, no doubt, in some cases, my dear fellow.

PODB. (*to* MISS T.). Do come and listen to him, most intelligent chap—great fun. Mr. Culchard is above that sort of thing, I dare say.

GUIDE. Your vriendts laike to choin, yais? Same for tree as for von. I exblain all de beecture.

MISS T. You're vurry obliging, Mr. Podbury, but your friend is explaining it all just splendidly.

PODB. (*piqued*). Perhaps I had better dismiss my chap, and take on Mr. Culchard too?

MISS T. No, I'd just hate to have you do that. Keep on going round. You mustn't mind us, indeed!

PODB. Oh, if you'd rather! (*Gloomily, to* GUIDE.) They can do without *us*. Just show me something more in the blood-and-thunder line—no, at the other end of the room. [*They withdraw.*

GUIDE. Hier is von dat is vary amusant. You know de schtory of de Tree Vishes, eh?

PODB. *Macbeth*, eh? oh, I see—*Wishes!* No, what was that?

GUIDE. I dell it you. (*He tells it;* PODBURY *falls into gloomy abstraction.*) ... And inschdantly she vind a grade pig soasage at de end of her noâse. So de ole voman——

PODB. (*wearily*). Oh, I've heard all *that*. What's this one about?

GUIDE. Dis is galled "De lasht Gannon." You see de vigure of Ceevilization flodderin op viz de vings, vile Brogress preaks asonder de lasht gon, and in a gorner a Genius purns de vrontier bosts.

PODB. (*captiously*). What's he doing *that* for?

Guide. I ton't know. I subbose begause dey are bosts, or (*dubiously*) begause he is a Genius.

Culch. (*touching* Podbury's *arm as he goes out*). Oh—er—Podbury, I'm off. Going to lunch somewhere with the—ah—Trotters. See you at *table d'hôte* this evening, I suppose? Good-bye.

Podb. (*savagely*). Oh, ta-ta! (*To himself.*) And that's the fellow who said he wanted to keep out of making friends! How the dickens am I going to get through the time by myself? (*To* Guide.) Here, that's enough for one day.

Guide. If you vandt to puy som real Prussels lace for your sweedardt, I——

Podb. (*grimly*). I've no occasion for any at present, thank you.

[*He pays and dismisses him, and stands forlornly in the Gallery, while the Imperfectly Educated Daughter goes on spelling out the Catalogue for her Parents' edification.*

CHAPTER V.
Culchard has the Best of it.

SCENE—*Upper deck of the Rhine Steamer*, König Wilhelm, *somewhere between Bonn and Bingen. The little tables on deck are occupied by English, American, and German tourists, drinking various liquids, from hock to Pilsener beer, and eating veal cutlets.* MR. CYRUS K. TROTTER *is on the lower deck, discussing the comparative merits of the New York hotels with a fellow countryman.* MISS MAUD S. TROTTER *is seated on the afterdeck in close conversation with* CULCHARD. PODBURY *is perched on a camp-stool in the forward part. Near him a British Matron, with a red-haired son, in a green and black blazer, and a blue flannel nightcap, and a bevy of rabbit-faced daughters, are patronising a tame German Student in spectacles, who speaks a little English.*

THE BRITISH MATRON. Oh, you *ought* to see London; it's our capital—chief city, you know. Very grand—large—four million inhabitants! [*With pride, as being in some way responsible for this.*

A RABBIT-FACED DAUGHTER (*with a simper*). Quite a little *world!*
    [*She looks down her nose, as if in fear of having said something a little too original.*

THE GERM. STUD. No, I haf not yet at London peen. Ven I vill pedder Englisch learn, I go.

THE BLAZER. You read our English books, I suppose? Dickens, you know, and Homer, eh? About the Trojan War—that's his *best* work!

THE STUD. (*Ollendorffically*). I haf not read Diggins; but I haf read ze bapers by *Bigvig.* Zey are vary indereshtin, and gurious.

A PATRIOTIC YOUNG SCOT (*to an admiring Elderly Lady in a black*
E

mushroom hat). Eh, but we just made a pairrty and went up Auld Drachenfels, and when we got to th' tope, we danced a richt gude Scots

MR. CYRUS K. TROTTER DISCUSSING NEW YORK HOTELS.

reel, and sang, "*We're a' togither an' naebody by*," concluding—just to show, ye'll understan', that we were loyal subjies—wi' "*God Save*

Culchard has the Best of It.

th' Queen." The peasants didna seem just to know what to mak' of us, I prawmise ye!

THE BLACK MUSHROOM. How I wish I'd been one of you!

THE YOUNG SCOT *(candidly)*. I doot your legs would ha' stood such wark.

[PODBURY *becomes restless, and picks his way among the camp-stools to* CULCHARD *and* MISS TROTTER.

PODBURY *(to himself)*. Time *I* had a look in, I think. *(Aloud.)* Well, Miss Trotter, what do you think of the Rhine, as far as you've got?

MISS T. Well, I guess it's navigable, as far as *I've* got.

PODB. No, but I mean to say—does it come up to the mark in the scenery line, you know?

MISS T. I cannt answer that till I know whereabouts it is they mark the scenery-line. I expect Mr. Culchard knows. He knows pretty well everything. Would you like to have him explain the scenery to you going along? His explanations are vurry improving, I assure you.

PODB. I dare say; but the scenery just here is so flat that even my friend's remarks won't improve it.

CULCH. *(producing his note-book ostentatiously)*. I do not propose to attempt it. No doubt you will be more successful in entertaining Miss Trotter than I can pretend to be. I retire in your favour. [*He scribbles.*

PODB. Is that our expenses you're corking down there, Culchard, eh?

CULCH. *(with dignity)*. If you want to know, I am "corking down," to adopt your elegant expression, a sonnet that suggested itself to me.

PODB. Much better cork that *up*, old chap—hadn't he, Miss Trotter?
[*He glances at her for appreciation.*

MISS T. That's so. I don't believe the poetic spirit has much chance of slopping over so long as Mr. Podbury is around. You have considerable merit as a stopper, Mr. Podbury.

PODB. I see; I'd better clear out till the poetry has all gurgled out of him, eh? Is that the idea?

MISS T. If it is, it's your own, so I guess it's a pretty good one.
[PODBURY *shoulders off.*

CULCH. (*with his pathetic stop on*). I wish I had more of your divine patience! Poor fellow, he is not without his good points; but I do find him a thorn in my flesh occasionally, I'm afraid.

MISS T. Well, I don't know as a thorn in the flesh is any the pleasanter for having a good point.

CULCH. Profoundly true, indeed. I often think I could like him better if there were less in him to like. I assure you he tries me so at times that I could almost wish I was back at work in my department at Somerset House!

MISS T. I dare say you have pretty good times there, too. Isn't that one of your leading dry goods stores?

CULCH. (*pained*). It is not; it is a Government Office, and I am in the Pigeonhole and Docket Department, with important duties to discharge. I hope you didn't imagine I sold ribbons and calico over a counter?

MISS T. (*ambiguously*). Well, I wasn't just sure. It takes a pretty bright man to do that where I come from.

AN OLD LADY (*who is sitting next to* PODBURY, *and reading a home-letter to another Old Lady*). "Dear Maria and dear Madeline are close by, they have taken very comfortable lodgings in Marine Crescent. Dear Madeline's frame is expected down next Saturday."

SECOND OLD LADY. Madeline's frame! Is anything wrong with the poor girl's spine?

FIRST OLD LADY. I never heard of it. Oh, I see, it's *fiancé*, my dear. Caroline *does* write so illegibly. (*Continuing.*) "Um—um,— suppose you know she will be maimed——" (perhaps it *is* her spine after all—oh, *married*, to be sure), "very slowly" (is it slowly or shortly, I wonder?), um, um, "very quiet wedding, nobody but dear Mr. Wilkinson and his hatter."

SECOND O. L. The idea of choosing one's hatter for one's best man! I'm surprised Maria should allow it!

FIRST O. L. Maria always *was* peculiar—still, now I come to look, it's more like "brother," which is certainly *much* more suitable. (*Continuing.*) "She will have no—no bird's-marks . . ." (Now, what *does* that—should you think that meant "crows-feet"? Oh, no, *how* stupid of me—*bridesmaids*, of course!)—"and will go to the otter a plain guy"— (Oh, Caroline really is *too* . . .)—"to the *altar* in plain *grey*! She has been given such quantities of pea-nuts"—(very odd things to give a girl! Oh, *presents!* um, um)—"Not settled yet where to go for their hangman"—(the officiating clergyman, I suppose—very flippant way of putting it, I *must* say! It's meant for *honeymoon*, though, I see, to be sure!) &c. &c.

CULCH. (*to* MISS T.). I should like to be at Nuremberg with you. It would be an unspeakable delight to watch the expansion of a fresh young soul in that rich mediæval atmosphere!

MISS T. I guess you'll have opportunities of watching Mr. Podbury's fresh young soul under those conditions, any way.

CULCH. It would not be at all the same thing—even if he—but you *do* think you're coming to Nuremberg, don't you?

MISS T. Well, it's this way. Poppa don't want to get fooling around any more one-horse towns than he can help, and he's got to be fixed up with the idea that Nuremberg is a prominent European sight before he drops everything to get there.

CULCH. I will undertake to interest him in Nuremberg. Fortunately, we are all getting off at Bingen, and going, curiously enough, to the same hotel. (*To himself.*) Confound that fellow Podbury, here he is *again!*

PODB. (*to himself, as he advances*). If she's carrying on with that fellow, Culchard, to provoke me, I'll soon show her how little I— (*Aloud.*) I say, old man, hope I'm not interrupting you, but I just want to speak to you for a minute, if Miss Trotter will excuse us. Is there any particular point in going as far as Bingen to-night, eh?

CULCH. (*resignedly*). As much as there is in not going farther than somewhere else, *I* should have thought.

PODB. Well, but look here—why not stop at Bacharach, and see what sort of a place it is?

CULCH. You forget that our time is limited if we're going to stick to our original route.

PODB. Yes, of course; mustn't waste any on the Rhine. Suppose we push on to Maintz to-night, and get the Rhine off our hands then? (*With a glance at* MISS TROTTER.) The sooner I've done with this steamer business the better!

MISS T. Well, Mr. Podbury, that's not a vurry complimentary remark to make before me!

PODB. We've seen so little of one another lately that it can hardly make much difference—to *either* of us—can it?

MISS T. Now I call that real kind, you're consoling me in advance!

THE STEWARD (*coming up*). De dickets dat I haf nod yed seen! (*examining* CULCHARD'S *coupons*). For Bingen—so?

CULCH. *I* am. This gentleman gets off—is it Bacharach or Maintz, Podbury?

PODB. (*sulkily*). Neither, as it happens. I'm for Bingen, too, as you won't go anywhere else. Though you *did* say when we started, that the advantage of travelling like this was that we could go on or stop just as the fancy took us!

CULCH. (*calmly*). I did, my dear Podbury. But it never occurred to me that the fancy would take you to get tired of a place before you got there!

PODB. (*as he walks forwards*). Hang that fellow! I know I shall punch his head some day. And She didn't seem to care whether I stayed or not. (*Hopefully.*) But you never *can* tell with women!

[*He returns to his camp-stool and the letter-reading Old Ladies.*

CHAPTER VI.

Culchard makes a little Miscalculation.

SCENE.—*Garden of the Hotel Victoria at Bingen, commanding a view of the Rhine and the vine-terraced hills, which are bathed in warm afternoon sunlight. Under the mopheaded acacias,* CULCHARD *and* PODBURY *are sitting smoking. At a little distance from them, are a Young Married Couple, whose honeymoon is apparently in its last quarter.*

THE BRIDEGROOM (*lazily, to Bride, as she draws another chair towards her for a foot-rest*). How many *more* chairs do you want?

BRIDE (*without looking at him*). I should think you could spare me one—you can hardly sit on three at once!

[*After this interchange of amenities, they consider themselves absolved from any further conversational efforts.*]

PODB. (*to* CULCH., *resuming a discussion*). I know as well as you do that we are booked for Nuremberg; but what *I* say is—that's no earthly reason why we should *go* there!

CULCH. No reason why *you* should go, unless you wish it, certainly. *I* intend to go.

PODB. Well, it's beastly selfish, that's all! I know *why* you're so keen about it, too. Because the Trotters are going.

CULCH. (*colouring*). That's an entire mistake on your part. Miss Trotter has nothing to do with it. I don't even know whether she's going or not—for certain.

PODB. No, but you've a pretty good idea that she *is*, though. And I *know* how it will be. You'll be going about with her all the time, and I shall be shunted on to the old man! I don't *see* it, you know! (CULCH. *remains silent. A pause.* PODBURY *suddenly begins to search his pockets.*)

I say—here's a pretty fix! Look here, old fellow, doosid annoying thing, but I can't find my purse—must have lost it somewhere!

CULCH. (*stoically*). I can't say I'm surprised to hear it. It's awkward, certainly. I suppose I shall have to lend you enough to go home with—it's all I can do; but I'll do that with—er—pleasure.

PODB. (*staring*). Go home? Why, I can wire to the governor for more, easily enough. We shall have to stay here till it comes, that's all.

CULCH. And give up Nuremberg? Thank you!

PODB. I rather like this place, you know—sort of rest. And we could always nip over to Ems, or Homburg, if it got too slow, eh?

CULCH. If I nip over anywhere, I shall nip to Nuremberg. We may just as well understand one another, Podbury. If I'm to provide money for both of us, it's only reasonable that you should be content to go where *I* choose. I cannot, and will not, stand these perpetual interferences with our original plan; it's sheer restlessness. Come with me to Nuremberg, and I shall be very happy to be your banker. Otherwise, you must stay here alone. [*He compresses his lips and crosses his legs.*

PODB. Oh, *that's* it, is it? But look here, why not tit up whether we go on or stay?

CULCH. Why should I "tit up," as you call it, when I've already made up my mind to go? When I once decide on anything, it's final.

THE BRIDE (*to Bridegroom, without enthusiasm*). Would you like me to roll you a cigarette?

BRIDEGROOM (*with the frankness of an open nature*). Not if I know it. I can do it better myself.

BRIDE (*coldly*). I see.

> [*Another silence, at the end of which she rises and walks slowly away, pausing at the gate to see whether he intends to follow. As he does not appear to have remarked her absence, she walks on.*

PODB. (*to* CULCH., *in an undertone*). I say, those two don't seem to hit it off exactly, eh? Seem sorry they came! You'll be glad to hear, old fellow, that we needn't separate after all. Just found my purse in my trouser-pocket!

Culchard makes a little Miscalculation.

CULCH. Better luck than you deserve. Didn't I tell you you should have a special pocket for your money and coupons? Like this—see. (*He opens his coat.*) With a buttoned flap, it stands to reason they *must* be safe!

"GOOD HEAVENS, IT—IT'S GONE!"

PODB. So long as you keep it buttoned, old chap,—which you don't seem to do!

CULCH. (*annoyed*). Pshaw! The button is a trifle too——'*feels pocket and turns pale*). Good Heavens, it—it's *gone!*

PODB. The button?

CULCH. (*patting himself all over with shaking hands*). Everything!—money, coupons, circular notes! They—they must have fallen out going up that infernal Niederwald. (*Angrily.*) You *would* insist on going!

PODB. Phew! The whole bag of tricks gone! You're lucky if you get them again. Any number of tramps and beggars all the way up. Shouldn't have taken off your coat—very careless of you! (*He grins.*)

CULCH. It was so hot. I must go and inform the Police here—I may recover it yet. Anyway, we—we must push on to Nuremberg, and I'll telegraph home for money to be sent here. You can let me have enough to get on with?

PODB. With all the pleasure in life, dear boy—on your own conditions, you know. I mean, if I pay the piper, I call the tune. Now, I don't cotton to Nuremberg somehow; I'd rather go straight on to Constance; we could get some rowing there.

CULCH. (*pettishly*). Rowing be——(*recollecting his helplessness*). No; but just consider, my dear Podbury. I assure you you'll find Nuremberg a most delightful old place. You must see how bent I am on going there!

PODB. Oh, yes, I see *that*. But then I'm *not*, don't you know—so there we are!

CULCH. (*desperately*). Well, I'll—I'll meet you half-way. I've no objection to—er—titting up with you—Nuremberg or Constance. Come?

PODB. You weren't so anxious to tit up just now—but never mind. (*Producing a mark.*) Now then, Emperor—Constance. Eagle—Nuremberg. Is it sudden death, or best out of three? [*He tosses.*

CULCH. Sud—— (*The coin falls with the Emperor uppermost.*) Best out of three. [*He takes coin from* PODBURY *and tosses.*

PODB. Eagle! we're even so far. (*He receives coin.*) This settles it. [*He tosses.*

CULCH. (*triumphantly*). Eagle again! Now mind, Podbury, no going back after *this*. It must *be* Nuremberg now.

PODB. All right! And now allow me to have the pleasure of restoring your pocket-book and note-case. They did fall out on the Niederwald, and it was a good job for you I was behind and saw them drop. You must really be careful, dear boy. Ain't you going to say "ta" for them?

Culchard makes a little Miscalculation.

CULCH. (*relieved*). I'm—er—tremendously obliged. I really can't say how.—(*Recollecting himself.*) But you need not have taken advantage of it to try to do me out of going to Nuremberg—it was a shabby trick!

PODB. Oh, it was only to get a rise out of you. I never meant to keep you to it, of course. And I say, weren't you sold, though? Didn't I lead up to it beautifully? (*He chuckles.*) Score to me, eh!

CULCH. (*with amiable sententiousness*). Ah, well, I don't grudge you your little joke if it amuses you. Those laugh best who laugh last. And it's settled now that we're going to Nuremberg.

[MISS TROTTER *and her father have come out from the Speisesaal doors, and overhear the last speech.*

MR. TROTTER (*to* CULCHARD). Your friend been gettin' off a joke on you, Sir?

CULCH. Only in his own estimation, Mr. Trotter. I have nailed him down to going to Nuremberg, which, for many reasons, I was extremely anxious to visit. (*Carelessly.*) Are we likely to be there when you are?

MISS T. I guess not. We've just got our mail, and my cousin, Charley Van Boodeler, writes he's having a real lovely time in the Engadine—says it's the most elegant locality he's struck yet, and just as full of Amurrcans as it can hold; so we're going to start out there right away. I don't believe we shall have time for Nuremberg this trip. Father, if we're going to see about checking the baggage through, we'd better go down to the *depôt* right now. [*They pass on.*

CULCH. (*with a very blank face and a feeble whistle*). Few-fitty-fitty-fitty-fa-di-fee-fee-foo; few——After all, Podbury, I don't know that I care so much about Nuremberg. They—they say it's a good deal changed from what it was.

PODB. So are *you*, old chap, if it comes to that. Tiddledy-iddlety-ido-lumpty-doodle-oo! Is it to be Constance after all, then?

CULCH. (*reddening*). Er—I rather thought of the Engadine—more bracing, eh?—few-feedle-eedle-oodle——

PODB. You artful old whistling oyster, *I* see what you're up to! But it's no go; she don't want either of us Engadining about after her. It's Charley Van Stickinthemud's turn now! We've got to go to Nuremberg.

You can't get out of it, after gassing so much about the place. When you've once decided, you know, it's *final!*

CULCH. (*with dignity*). I am not aware that I *wanted* to get out of it. I merely proposed in your——(PODBURY *suddenly explodes.*) What are you cackling at *now?*

PODB. (*wiping his eyes*). It's the last laugh, old man,—and it's the best!

> [CULCHARD *walks away rapidly, leaving* PODBURY *in solitary enjoyment of the joke.* PODBURY'S *mirth immediately subsides into gravity, and he kicks several unoffending chairs with quite uncalled-for brutality*.

CHAPTER VII.
A Dissolution of Partnership.

SCENE—*A Second-Class Compartment on the line between Wurzburg and Nuremberg.* PODBURY *has been dull and depressed all day, not having recovered from the parting with* MISS TROTTER. CULCHARD, *on the contrary, is almost ostentatiously cheerful.* PODBURY *is intensely anxious to find out how far his spirits are genuine, but—partly from shyness, and partly because some of their fellow travellers have been English—he has hesitated to introduce the subject. At last, however, they are alone, and he is determined to have it out on the very first opportunity.*

CULCHARD. Abominably slow train, this *Schnell-zug.* I hope we shall get to Nuremberg before it's too dark to see the general effect.

PODBURY. We're not likely to be in time for *table d'hôte*—not that *I'm* peckish. (*He sighs.*) Wonder whereabouts the—the Trotters have got to by now, eh?

[*He feels he is getting red, and hums the Garden Scene from "Faust."*

CULCH. (*indifferently*). Oh, let me see—just arriving at St. Moritz, I expect. Wonderful effect of colour, that is.

[*He indicates the West, where a bar of crimson is flaming between a belt of firs.*

PODB. (*absently*). Oh, wonderful!—where? (*Hums a snatch of a waltz.*) Dum-dum-diddle-um-tum-dum-dum-dum-ty-doodle; dum-dum—I say, *you* don't seem particularly cut up?

CULCH. Cut up? Why should I be cut up, my dear fellow?—about what?

[*Before* PODBURY *can explain, two Talkative British Tourists tumble up into the compartment, and he has to control his curiosity once more.*

The Travelling Companions.

FIRST T. T. Well, I 'ope we're all right *now*, Sam, I'm sure—these German jokers have chivied us about enough for one journey! (*To* CULCHARD.) Not in your way, this 'at box, Sir? Don't give yer much

"PUTS ME IN MIND O' THE BEST PART O' BOX 'ILL."

space in these foreign trains. (*They settle down and the train starts.*) Pretty bit o' country along 'ere!—puts me in mind o' the best part o' Box 'Ill—and I can't say more for it than *that!*

SECOND T. T. (*a little man with a sandy fringe and boiled-looking eyes*).

A Dissolution of Partnership.

What I notice about the country abroad is they don't seem to 'ave no *landmarks*.

FIRST T. T. (*with a dash of friendly contempt*). What d'yer mean—no landmarks—*signposts*?

SECOND T. T. (*with dignity*). I mean to say, they don't 'ave nothing to indicate which is Jack's property, and which is Joe's.

FIRST T. T. Go on—they've as much as what *we* 'ave.

SECOND T. T. '*Ave* they? We 'ave fences and 'edges. I don't see none '*ere*. P'raps you'll point me *out* one?

FIRST T. T. There's precious few 'edges or fences in the Isle o' Thanet, as you'd know if you've ever been to Margit.

SECOND T. T. (*loftily*). I'm not talkin' about Margit now, I'm talkin' of 'ere, and I'll trouble you to show me a landmark.

FIRST T. T. Depend on it they've their own ways of knowing which is 'oo's.

SECOND T. T. That's not what I'm *sayin'*. I'm sayin' there ain't nothin' to *indicate* it. [*They argue the point at length.*

PODB. (*to* CULCHARD). Then you really aren't cut up—about Miss T. you know?

CULCH. (*with the reserve of a man who only wants to be pressed*). There is no reason that I'm aware of, why I should be—but (*lowering his voice*) don't you think we had better wait till we are alone to discuss that subject?

PODB. Oh, all right. I'm not partic—at least. Well, I'm glad you *aren't*, you know, that's all.

[*He becomes silent again—but his face brightens visibly.*

FIRST T. T. (*to Second Do.*). See that field there? That's tobacco, *that* is.

SECOND T. T. What they make their penny smokes of. (*The train enters a station.*) What funny engines they do 'ave 'ere! I expect the guard 'll be wanting to see our *billyetts* again next. It's as bad as it used to be with the passports. I've 'eard—mind yer, I don't know 'ow much likeli'ood there is in the assertion—that they're going to bring 'em in again. Most intricate they were about them. (*To* CULCHARD). Why, if you'll believe me, a friend o' mine as 'ad one—well, they got 'is description down to a ioter? He'd a cast in 'is eye,—they put it down, and a pimple you'd 'ardly notice—but down *that* went!

FIRST T. T. It's no use 'aving such things if they don't do it thoroughly.

SECOND T. T. (*irrelevantly*). I wish I 'adn't 'ad that glass o' peach wine where we changed last. (*A Guard appears at the window, and makes some guttural comments on the couple's tickets.*) Wechseln? Why, that means *wash*, don't it? I'm as clean as *him*, anyway. "Anshteigen,"—ah, I ought to know what *that* means by this time! Sam, my boy, we're bundled out again. I told yer 'ow it would be!

[*They tumble out, and the carriage is presently filled by an assortment of Germans, including a lively and sociable little Cripple with a new drinking-mug which he has just had filled with lager, and a Lady with pale hair and sentimental blue eyes.*

PODB. We can talk all right *now*, eh? *They* won't understand. Look here, old fellow, I don't mind owning *I'm* rather down in the mouth about——you know what. I shouldn't care so much if there was any chance of our coming across them again.

CULCH. (*cordially*). I am very glad to hear you say so. I was rather afraid you had taken a dislike—er—in that quarter.

PODB. I?—is it *likely!* I—I admire her awfully, you know, only she rather seemed to snub me lately.

CULCH. (*with patronising reassurance*). Quite a mistake on your part, I assure you, my dear fellow. I am sure she will learn to appreciate you—er—fully when you meet again, which, I may tell you, will be at no very distant date. I happen to know that she will be at the Italian Lakes next month, and so shall we, if you let me manage this tour my own way.

PODB. (*with surprise and gratitude*). I say, old boy, I'd no notion you were such a nailing good chap? Nein, danky. (*To the little Cripple, who is cheerily inviting him, in pantomime, to drink from his mug.*) Cheeky little beggar. But do you really think anything will—er—come of it, if we do meet her again—*do* you now?

CULCH. I—ah—have the best reasons for feeling tolerably certain of it. [*He looks out of window and smiles.*

A Dissolution of Partnership.

PODB. But that cousin of hers—Charley, you know—how about *him*?

CULCH. I put that to her, and there is nothing in it. In fact, she practically admitted—(*He glances round and lowers his voice.*) I will tell you another time. That lady over there is looking at us, and I'm almost certain——

PODB. What if she is, she don't understand a word we're saying. I want to hear all about Her, you know.

CULCH. My dear Podbury, we shall have ample time to talk about her while we are at Nuremberg together—it will be the greatest pleasure to me to do so as long as you please.

PODB. Thanks, old chap! I'd no idea you were doing all this, you know. But just tell me this, what did she *say* about me?

CULCH. (*mystified*). About you? I really don't recollect that she mentioned *you* particularly.

PODB. (*puzzled*). But I thought you said you'd been speaking up for me! What *did* you talk about then?

CULCH. Well, about myself—naturally.

[*He settles his collar with a vague satisfaction.*

PODB. (*blankly*). Oh! Then you haven't been arranging to meet her again on *my* account?

CULCH. Good Heavens, no—what a very grotesque idea of yours, my dear fellow! [*He laughs gently.*

PODB. Is it? You always gave out that she wasn't your style at all, and you only regarded her as a "study," and rot like that. How could *I* tell you would go and cut me out?

CULCH. I don't deny that she occasionally—er—jarred. She is a little deficient in surface refinement—but that will come, that will come. And as to "cutting you out," why, you must allow you never had the remotest——

PODB. I don't allow anything of the sort. She liked me well enough till—till you came in and set her against me, and you may think it friendly if you like, but I call it shabby—confoundedly shabby.

CULCH. Don't talk so loud, I'm sure I saw that woman smile!

PODB. She may smile her head off for all I care. (*The train stops;*

the Cripple and all but the Pale-haired Lady *get out.*) Here we are at Nuremberg. What hotel did you say you are going to?
   CULCH. The Bayrischer-Hof. Why?
            [*He gets his coat and stick, &c., out of the rack.*
   PODB. Because I shall go to some other, that's all.
   CULCH. (*in dismay*). My dear Podbury, this is really too childish! There's no sense in travelling together, if we're going to stay at different hotels!
   PODB. I'm not sure I shall go any further. Anyway, while I *am* here, I prefer to keep to myself.
   CULCH. (*with a displeased laugh*). Just as you please. It's a matter of perfect indifference to *me*. I'm afraid you'll be terribly bored by yourself, though.
   PODB. That's *my* look out. It can't be worse than going about with you and listening while you crow and drivel about *her*, that's one comfort! [*The* Pale-haired Lady *coughs in a suspicious manner.*
   CULCH. You don't even know if there *is* another hotel.
   PODB. I don't care. I can find a pot-house somewhere, I daresay.
   THE PALE-HAIRED LADY (*in excellent English, to* PODBURY *as he passes out*). Pardon me, you will find close to the Bahnhof a very goot hotel—the Wurtemburger.
      [PODBURY *thanks her and alights in some confusion; the* Lady *sinks back, smiling.*
   CULCH. (*annoyed*). She must have understood every word we said! Are you in earnest over this? (PODBURY *nods grimly.*) Well, you'll soon get tired of your own society, I warn you.
   PODB. Thanks, we shall see.
      [*He saunters off with his bag;* CULCHARD *shrugs his shoulders, and goes in search of the Bayrischer-Hof Porter, to whom he entrusts his luggage tickets, and takes his seat in the omnibus alone.*

CHAPTER VIII.

Podbury finds Consolation.

SCENE—*A Bridge over the Pegnitz, at Nuremberg. Time, afternoon. The shadows of the old gabled and balconied houses are thrown sharply on the reddish-yellow water. Above the steep speckled roofs, the spires of St. Lorenz glitter against the blue sky.* CULCHARD *is leaning listlessly upon the parapet of the bridge.*

CULCHARD (*to himself*). How mediæval it all is, and how infinitely restful! (*He yawns.*) What a blessed relief to be without that fellow Podbury! He's very careful to keep out of my way—I've scarcely seen him since I've been here. He must find it dreadfully dull. (*He sighs.*) I ought to find material for a colour-sonnet here, with these subdued grey tones, those dull coppery-greens, and the glowing reds of the conical caps of those towers. I *ought*—but I don't. I fancy that half-engagement to Maud Trotter must have scared away the Muse. I wonder if Podbury has really gone yet? (*Here a thump on the back disposes of any doubt as to this.*) Er—so you're still at Nuremberg? [*Awkwardly.*

PODB. (*cheerfully*). Rather! Regular ripping old place this—suits me down to the ground. And how are *you* getting on, my bonnie boy, eh?

CULCH. (*who does not quite like being addressed as a bonnie boy*). Perfectly, thanks. My mind is being—er—stimulated here in the direction most congenial to it.

PODB. So's mine. By the way, have you got a book—I don't mean a novel, but a regular improving book—the stodgier the better—to lend a fellow?

CULCH. Well, I brought an *Epitome of Herbert Spencer's Synthetic*

Philosophy away with me to dip into occasionally. It seems a very able summary, and you are welcome to it, if it's of any use to you.

PODB. Spencer, eh?—he's a stiff kind of old bird, ain't he? He'll do me to-rights, thanks.

CULCH. It strikes me, Podbury, that you must find the time rather long, to want a book of that kind. If you wish to resume our—ah—original relations, I am quite ready to overlook what I am sure was only a phase of not unnatural disappointment.

PODB. (*cheerfully*). Oh, *that's* all right, old fellow. I've got over all that business. (*He colours slightly.*) How soon did you think of moving on?

CULCH. (*briskly*). As soon as you please. We might start for Constance to-morrow, if you like.

PODB. (*hesitating*). Well, you see, it's just this: there's a fellow staying at my hotel—Prendergast, his name is—rattling good sort—and I've rather chummed up with him, and—and he's travelling with a relation of his, and—well, the fact is, they rather made a point of my going on to Constance with *them*, don't you see? But I daresay we could work it so as to go on all together. I'll see what they say about it.

CULCH. (*stiffly*). I'm exceedingly obliged—but so large a party is scarcely—however, I'll let you know whether I can join you or not this evening. Are you—er—going anywhere in particular just now?

PODB. Well, yes. I've got to meet Prendergast at the *Café Noris*. We're going to beat up some stables, and see if we can't hire a couple of gees for an hour or two before dinner. Do you feel inclined for a tittup?

CULCH. Thanks, but I am no equestrian. (*To himself, after* POD-BURY'S *departure.*) He seems to manage well enough without me. And yet I do think my society would be more good for him than——. Why did he want to borrow that book, though? Can my influence after all——(*He walks on thoughtfully, till he finds himself before an optician's window in which a mechanical monkey is looking through a miniature telescope; the monkey suddenly turns its head and gibbers at him. This familiarity depresses him, and he moves away, feeling lonelier than ever.*)

Podbury finds Consolation.

ON THE TERRACE OF THE BURG. HALF AN HOUR LATER.

CULCH. (*on a seat commanding a panorama of roofs, gables, turrets, and spires*). Now this is a thing that can only be properly enjoyed when one is by oneself. The mere presence of Podbury—well, thank goodness, he's found more congenial company. (*He sighs.*) That looks like an English girl sketching on the next seat. Rather a fine profile, so regular—general air of repose about her. Singular, now I think of it, how little repose there is about Maud. (*The Young Lady rises and walks to the parapet.*) Dear me, she has left her india-rubber behind her. I really think I ought—— (*He rescues the india-rubber, which he restores to the owner.*) Am I mistaken in supposing that this piece of india-rubber is your property?

THE Y. L. (*in musically precise tones*). Your supposition is perfectly correct. I was under the impression that it would be safe where it was for a few moments; but I am obliged to you, nevertheless. I find india-rubber quite indispensable in sketching.

CULCH. I can quite understand that. I—I mean that it reduces the —er—paralysing sense of irrevocability.

THE Y. L. You express my own meaning exactly.

[CULCHARD, *not being quite sure of his own, is proportionately pleased.*

CULCH. You have chosen an inspiring scene, rich with historical interest.

THE Y. L. (*enthusiastically*). Yes, indeed. What names rise to one's mind instinctively! Melanchthon, John Huss, Kraft, and Peter Vischer, and Dürer, and Wohlgemut, and Maximilian the First, and Louis of Bavaria!

CULCH. (*who has read up the local history, and does not intend to be beaten at this game*). Precisely. And the imperious Margrave of Brandenburg, and Wallenstein, and Gustavus Adolphus, and Goetz von Berlichingen. One can almost see their—er—picturesque personalities still haunting the narrow streets as we look down.

THE Y. L. I find it impossible to distinguish even the streets from here, I confess, but you probably see with the imagination of an artist. *Are* you one by any chance?

CULCH. Only in words; that is, I record my impressions in a poetic

"ER—I HAVE BROUGHT YOU THE PHILOSOPHICAL WORK I MENTIONED."

form. A perfect sonnet may render a scene, a mood, a passing thought, more indelibly than the most finished sketch; may it not?

THE Y. L. That is quite true; indeed, I occasionally relieve my feelings by the composition of Greek or Latin verses, which I find, on the whole, better adapted to express the subtler emotions. Don't you agree with me there?

Podbury finds Consolation.

CULCH. (*who has done no Greek or Latin verse since he left school*). Doubtless. But I am hindering your sketch?

THE Y. L. No, I was merely saturating my mind with the general effect. I shall not really begin my sketch till to-morrow. I am going now. I hope the genius of the place will inspire you.

CULCH. Thank you. I trust it will—er—have that effect. (*To himself, after the* Young Lady *has left the terrace*.) Now, that's a very superior girl—she has intellect, style, culture—everything the ideal woman *should* have. I wonder, now, whether, if I had met her before—but such speculations are most unprofitable! How clear her eyes looked through her *pince-nez!* Blue-grey, like Athene's own. If I'd been with Podbury, I should never have had this talk. The sight of him would have repelled her at once. I shall tell him when I take him that book that he had better go his own way with his new friends. I like the view from this terrace—I shall come up here again—often.

SCENE—*The Conversations-Saal at the Wurtemburger-Hof. Evening.* PODBURY *at the piano;* BOB PRENDERGAST *and his sister* HYPATIA *seated near him.*

PODB. (*chanting dolefully*)—

> Now then, this party as what came from Fla-an-ders,
> What had the com-plex-i-on rich and rare,
> He went and took and caught the yaller ja-un-ders—
> And his complexion isn't what it were!

MR. AND MISS PRENDERGAST (*joining sympathetically in chorus*). And his complexion *isn't* what it *were!*

[*There is a faint knock at the door, and* CULCHARD *enters with a volume under his arm. None of the three observe him, and he stands and listens stiffly as* PODBURY *continues,—*

> Well, next this party as what came from Fla-an ders,
> Whose complex-shun was formi-ally rare,
> Eloped to Injia with Eliza Sa-aun-ders,
> As lived close by in Canonbury Square.

CULCH. (*advances to piano and touches* PODBURY'S *arm with the air of his better angel*). Er—I have brought you the philosophical work I mentioned. I will leave it for an occasion when you are—er—in a fitter frame of mind for its perusal.

PODB. Oh, beg pardon, didn't see you, old fellow. Awfully obliged; jam it down anywhere, and (*whispering*) I say, I want to introduce you to——

CULCH. (*in a tone of emphatic disapproval*). You must really excuse me, as I fear I should be scarcely a congenial spirit in such a party. So good-night—or, rather—er—good-*bye*. [*He withdraws.*

MISS HYPATIA P. (*just as* C. *is about to close the door*). Please don't stop, Mr. Podbury, that song is quite too deliciously inane!

[CULCHARD *turns as he hears the voice, and—too late—recognises his Athene of that afternoon. He retires in confusion, and, as he passes under the window, hears* PODBURY *sing the final verse.*

> The moral is—Now *don't* you come from Fla-an-ders,
> If you should have complexions rich and rare;
> And don't you go and catch the yaller ja-aun-ders,
> Nor yet know girls in Canonbury Square!

MISS HYPATIA P. (*in a clear soprano*). "Nor yet know girls in Canonbury Square!" [CULCHARD *passes on, crushed.*

CHAPTER IX.

Culchard is rather too Clever.

SCENE—*The Burg Terrace at Nuremberg.* PODBURY *on a bench, grappling with the "Epitome of Spencer."*

PODB. (*reading aloud, with comments*). "For really to conceive the infinite divisibility of matter is mentally to follow out the divisions to infinity, and to do this would require infinite time." You're right *there*, old cock, and, as I haven't got it to spare, I won't trouble you!—um—um . . . "opposite absurdities"—"subjective modifications" . . . "ultimate scientific ideas, then, are all representative of ideas that cannot be comprehended." I could have told *him* that. What bally rot this Philosophy is—but I suppose I must peg away at it. Didn't she say she was sorry I didn't go in more for cultivating my mind? (*He looks up.*) Jove, here she comes! and yes, there's that beggar Culchard with her! I thought he'd—how the dickens did he manage to——? I see what *he's* after—thinks he'll cut me out—twice over—but he shan't this time, if I can help it.

CULCH. (*to* MISS HYPATIA PRENDERGAST). No, the Modern Spirit is too earnestly intent upon solving the problems of existence to tolerate humour in its literature. Humour has served a certain purpose in its day, but that day is done, and I for one cannot pretend to regret its decay.

MISS H. P. Nor I. In fact, the only humour I ever *really* appreciated is that of the ancient classics. There has been no true fun since Aristophanes died. At least, *I* think not.

PODB. (*catching the last sentence*). Oh, I say, come, Miss Prendergast. Have you ever read *The Jumping Frog?*

PODBURY GRAPPLING WITH THE EPITOME OF SPENCER.

Miss P. And are you not enchanted by the logical lucidity of that great thinker?

Podb. Um—I should be more enchanted if I ever had the faintest notion what the great thinker was driving at. Look here—here's a simple little sentence for you! (*Reads.*) "Let us therefore bear in mind the following:—That of the whole incident force affecting an aggregate, the effective force is that which remains after deducting the non-effective, that the temporarily effective and the permanently effective vary inversely, and that the molar and molecular changes wrought by the permanently

Culchard is Rather too Clever.

effective force also vary inversely." (*With pathos.*) And that's only in an *Epitome*, mind you!

Miss P. Really, Mr. Podbury, I see nothing particularly incomprehensible in that.

Culch. (*with his superior smile*). My dear Podbury, you can hardly expect to master the Spencerian phraseology and habit of thought without at least *some* preliminary mental discipline!

Podb. (*nettled*). Oh—but *you* find him plain-sailing enough, I suppose?

Culch. I have certainly not encountered any insuperable difficulties in his works as *yet*.

Podb. Well, I'll just trouble you to explain *this*—wait a bit. (*Opens volume again.*) Ah, here we are—"And these illusive and primordial cognitions, or pseud-ideas, are homogeneous entities which may be differentiated objectively or subjectively, according as they are presented as Noumenon or Phenomenon. Or, in other words, they are only cognoscible as a colligation of incongruous coalescences." Now then—are you going to tell me you can make head or tail of all that?

Culch. (*perceiving that* Miss P. *is awaiting his reply in manifest suspense*). It's simple enough, my dear fellow, only I can't expect *you* to grasp it. It is merely a profound truth stated with masterly precision.

Podb. Oh, is *that* all, my dear fellow? (*He flings up his heels in an ecstasy.*) I *knew* I'd have you! Why, I made that up myself as I went along, and if *you* understand it, it's a jolly sight more than *I* do!

[*He roars with laughter.*

Miss P. (*behind her handkerchief*). Mr. Culchard has evidently gone through the—the "preliminary mental discipline."

Culch. (*scarlet and sulky*). Of course, if Mr. Podbury descends to childishness of that sort, I can't pretend to——

Podb. (*wiping his eyes*). But you *did* pretend, old chap. You said it was "profound truth" and "masterly precision"! I've got more profound truth where *that* came from. I say, I shall set up as an intellectual Johnny after this, and get you to write an Epitome of me. I think I pulled your leg *that* time, eh?

Culch. (*biting his lip*). When you have extracted sufficient entertainment from that very small joke, you will perhaps allow Miss Prendergast to sit down and begin her sketch. You may not be aware that you've taken her place.

[*He withdraws majestically to the parapet, while* PODBURY *makes way for* MISS P. *with apologies.*

PODB. (*as he leans over seat while she sketches*). I wish your brother Bob had been here—he would have enjoyed that!

MISS P. It was really too bad of you, though. Poor Mr. Culchard!

PODB. He shouldn't try to make me out a bigger duffer than I am, then. But I say, you don't *really* think it was too bad? Ah, you're *laughing*—you don't!

MISS P. Never mind what I really think. But you have got us both into sad disgrace. Mr. Culchard is dreadfully annoyed with us—look at his *shoulders!*

CULCH. (*leaning over parapet with his back to them*). That *ass* Podbury! To think of his taking me in with an idiotic trick like that! And before Her too! And when I had made it all right about the other evening, and was producing an excellent impression on the way up here. I wish I could hear what they are whispering about—more silly jokes at my expense, no doubt. Bah! as if it affected *me!*

PODB. (*to* MISS P.). I say, how awfully well you draw!

MISS P. There you betray your ignorance in Art matters. Sketching with me is a pastime, not a serious pursuit. (*They go on conversing in a lower tone.*) No, *please*, Mr. Podbury. I'm quite sure he would never——

PODB. (*rises; comes up to* CULCHARD, *and touches his shoulder*). I say, old chappie——

CULCH. (*jerking away with temper*). Now, look here, Podbury. I'm not in the mood for any more of your foolery——

PODB. (*humbly*). All right, old boy. I wouldn't bother you, only Miss Prendergast wants a figure for her foreground, and I said I'd ask you if you'd keep just as you are for a few minutes. Do you mind?

CULCH. (*to himself*). Afraid she's gone too far—thinks she'll smooth me down! Upon my word, it would serve her right to—but no, I won't be

Culchard is Rather too Clever. 53

petty. (*Aloud.*) Pray tell Miss Prendergast that I have no immediate intention of altering my position.

PODB. Thanks awfully, old chap. I knew you'd oblige.

CULCH. (*incisively*). I am obliging Miss Prendergast, and her only. (*Raising his voice, without turning his head.*) Would you prefer me to *face* you, Miss Prendergast?

MISS P. (*in tremulous tones*). N—no, thank you. It—it's so much more n—natural, don't you know, for you to be I—looking at the view.

CULCH. As you please. (*To himself.*) Can't meet my eye. Good! I shall go on treating her distantly for a little. I wonder if I look indifferent enough from behind? Shall I cross one foot? Better not—she may have begun sketching me. If she imagines I'm susceptible to feminine flattery of this palpable kind, she'll ——how her voice shook, though, when she spoke. Poor girl, she's afraid she offended me by laughing—and I *did* think she had more sense than to—but I mustn't be too hard on her. I'm afraid she's already beginning to think too much of—and with my peculiar position with Miss Trotter—(Maud, that is)—not that there's anything definite at present, still——(*Aloud.*) Ahem, Miss Prendergast—am I standing as you wish? (*To himself.*) She doesn't answer—too absorbed, and I can't hear that idiot—found he hasn't scored so much after all, and gone off in a huff, I expect. So much the better! What a time she is over this, and how quiet she keeps! I wish I knew whether it was coquetry or—shall I turn round and see? No, I must be perfectly indifferent. And she *did* laugh at me. I distinctly saw her. Still, if she's sorry, this would be an excellent opportunity for—(*Aloud.*) Miss Prendergast! (*No reply— —louder.*) May I take it that you regret having been betrayed into momentary approbation of a miserable piece of flippancy? If so, let me assure you—(*Turns round—to discover that he is addressing two little flaxen haired girls in speckled pinafores, who are regarding him open-mouthed.* MISS PRENDERGAST *and* PODBURY *have disappeared.*) Podbury *again!* He must have planned this—with *her!* It is too much. I have done— yes—done with the pair of them! [*Strides off in bitter indignation.*

CHAPTER X.

𝔓obbury insists on an 𝔈xplanation.

SCENE—*A flight of steps by the lake in the grounds of the Insel Hôtel, Constance. Time, late afternoon. A small boat, containing three persons, is just visible far out on the glassy grey-green water.* BOB PRENDERGAST *and* PODBURY *are perched side by side on a parapet, smoking disconsolately.*

PODBURY. Do they look at all as if they meant to come in? I tell you what, Bob, I vote we row out to them and tell them they'll be late for *table d'hôte*. Eh? [*He knocks out his pipe.*

PRENDERGAST (*phlegmatically*). Only be late for it ourselves if we do. They'll come in when they want to.

PODB. It's not safe for your sister,—I'm hanged if it is—going out in a boat with a duffer like Culchard! He'll upset her as sure as eggs.

PREND. (*with fraternal serenity*). With pin-oars? Couldn't if he tried! And they've a man with them, too. The less I see of that chap Culchard the better. I did hope we'd choked him off at Nuremberg. I hate the sight of his supercilious old mug!

PODB. You can't hate it more than I do—but what can I do? (*Pathetically.*) I've tried rotting him, but somehow he always manages to get the best of it in the end. I never saw such a beggar to hang on!

PREND. What on earth made you ask him to come on here, after he declared he wouldn't?

PODB. I! *I* ask him? He settled it all with your sister. How could *I* help it?

PREND. I'd do *something*. Why can't you tell him right out he ain't wanted? *I* would—like a shot!

PODB. It's not so easy to tell him as you think. We haven't been on speaking terms these three days. And, after all (*feebly*) we're supposed to be travelling together, don't you know! *You* might drop him a hint now.

PREND. Don't see how I can very well—not on my own hook. Might lead to ructions with Hypatia, too.

PODB. (*anxiously*). Bob, you—you don't think your sister really ——eh?

PREND. Hypatia's a rum girl—always was. She certainly don't seem to object to your friend Culchard. What the dickens she can see in him, I don't know!—but it's no use my putting *my* oar in. She'd only jump on *me*, y'know!

PODB. (*rising*). Then I *must*. If that's what he's really after, I think I can stop his little game. I'll try, at any rate. It's a long worm that has no turning, and I've had about enough of it. The first chance I get, I'll go for him.

PREND. Good luck to you, old chap. There, they're coming in now. We'd better go in and change, eh? We've none too much time.

[*They go in.*

In the Lese-zimmer, a small gaslit room, with glazed doors opening upon the Musik-saal. Around a table piled with German and English periodicals, a mild Curate, the Wife of the English Chaplain, and two Old Maids are seated, reading and conversing. CULCHARD *is on a central ottoman, conscientiously deciphering the jokes in "Fliegende Blätter."* PODBURY *is at the bookcase, turning over odd Tauchnitz volumes.*

THE CHAPLAIN'S WIFE (*to the* CURATE, *a new arrival*). Oh, you will *very* soon get into all our little ways. The hours here are *most* convenient —breakfast (*table d'hôte*) with choice of eggs or fish and coffee—really *admirable* coffee—from eight to nine; midday dinner at one. Supper at nine. Then, if you want to write a letter, the post for England goes out —(*&c., &c.*) And on Sundays, eleven o'clock service (Evangelical, of course!) at the —— (*&c., &c.,*) My husband—— (*&c., &c.*)

FIRST OLD MAID (*looking up from a four days' old "Telegraph"*). I see they are still continuing that very interesting correspondence on "Our Children's Mouths—and are they widening?" One letter attributes it to the habit of thumb-sucking in infancy—which certainly ought to be checked. Now I never *would* allow any——

THE C.'S. W. Nor I. But corals are quite as bad. Only this afternoon I was telling a Lady in this hotel that her little boy would be much happier with a rubber ring. You get them at a shop in the Hoch-strasse—I can take you to it at any time, or if you like to mention my name—— (*&c., &c.*)

SECOND O. M. One correspondent thought the practice of eating soup with table-spoons tended to enlarge the mouth. I really believe there may be something in it. [*A pause.*

THE CURATE. The weather we have been having seems to have materially affected the harvest prospects at home; they say there will be little or no fodder for the cattle this year. I saw somewhere—I forget where it was exactly—a suggestion to feed cows on chickweed.

PODB. (*at the bookcase*). Capital thing for them too, Sir. Know a man who never gives his cattle anything else.

THE CURATE. Oh, really? And does he find the experiment answer?

PODB. They take to it like birds. And—curious thing—after he'd tried it a month, all the cows turned yellow and went about chirping and twittering and hopping. Fact, I assure you!

THE CURATE. Dear me—I should scarcely have——

[*He gradually comes to the conclusion that he is being trifled with, and after a few moments of uncomfortable silence, gets up and quits the room with dignity.*

PODB. (*to himself*). One of 'em gone! Now if I can only clear these old tabbies out, I can tackle Culchard. (*Aloud, to* CHAPLAIN'S WIFE.) You don't happen to know if there's a good doctor here, I suppose?

Podbury insists on an Explanation. 57

A lady was saying in the Musik-saal—the lady with the three daughters who came this afternoon—that she was afraid they were in for bad feverish colds or something, and asking who there was to call in.

GETS UP AND QUITS THE ROOM WITH DIGNITY.

THE C.'S W. Oh, I've *no* belief in foreign doctors. I always find a few drops of aconite or pulsatilla.——I have my homœopathic case with me now. Perhaps, if I went and had a talk with her I could——

[*She goes out energetically.*

PODB. Another gone! (*To the* OLD MAIDS. So you aren't going down to the Cloisters to-night? I'm told there's to be some fun there—Hide-and-seek, or something—first-rate place for it, especially now the moon's up!

FIRST O. M. Nobody told *us* a word about it. Hide-and-seek

—and in those quaint old Cloisters too—It sounds delightful! What do you say, Tabitha. Shall we just——? Only to look *on*, you know. We needn't *play*, unless——

[*The* TWO OLD MAIDS *withdraw in a pleased flutter.* PODBURY *crosses to* CULCHARD.

PODB. (*with determination*). Look here, Culchard, I'd just like to know what you mean by the way you're going on.

CULCH. I thought we were both agreed that discussions of this kind——

PODB. It's all bosh our travelling together if we're not to have any discussions. You've been on the sulk long enough. And I'll thank you to inform me what you're after here, going about alone with Miss Prendergast like this, in the Museum with her all the morning, and on the lake again this afternoon—it won't *do*, you know!

CULCH. If she happens to prefer my society to yours and her brother's, I presume you have no claim to interfere.

PODB. I don't know about that. How about Miss Trotter?

CULCH. If I remember rightly, you yourself were not insensible to Miss Trotter's—er—attractions?

PODB. Perhaps not; but I am not engaged to her—you *are*. You told me so in the train.

CULCH. You entirely misunderstood me. There was no definite understanding between us—nothing of the sort or kind. In fact, it was merely a passing caprice. Since I have had the privilege of knowing Miss Prendergast, I see clearly——

PODB. Then you mean to propose to her, eh?

CULCH. That is certainly my intention; have you any objection to offer?

PODB. Only that I mean to propose too. I dare say my chances are as good as yours—even now.

CULCH. I doubt it, my dear fellow; however, don't let *me* discourage you.

PODB. I don't intend to. (*The figure of* MISS PRENDERGAST *is seen to pass the glazed doors, and move slowly across the Musik-saal; both rush*

Podbury insists on an Explanation.

to the door, and look after her.) She's gone out into the balcony. 'Jove, I'll go too, and get it over!

CULCH. I should not advise you to do so. It is possible she may have gone there with the—er—expectation of being joined by—by somebody else. [*He smiles complacently.*

PODB. You mean she gave you a *rendezvous* there? I don't believe it!

CULCH. I did not say so. But I am not prepared to deny that I have been waiting here with some such expectation.

PODB. (*holding the door*). If you go, I go too—that's all.

CULCH. Don't be absurd. You will only be *de trop*, I assure you.

PODB. *De trop* or not, I mean going—she shall choose between us.

CULCH. (*turning pale*). I suppose you intend to enlighten her as to my—er—little flirtation (before I knew *her*) with Miss Trotter? Do it, Podbury, do it—if you think you'll gain any good by it!

PODB. Telling tales is not exactly in my line. But you don't go on that balcony without me—that's all.

CULCH. Well, listen to reason, my dear fellow. What you propose is ridiculous. I—I don't mind conceding this: we'll each go, and—er—tit up, as you call it, which goes first.

PODB. Done with you! (*Produces a mark.*) Sudden death. You're Eagle—I'm the other Johnny. (*Tosses.*) Eagle! Confound you! But I mean to have my innings all the same.

CULCH. You're perfectly welcome—when I've had mine. I'll—er—wish you good evening.

[*He stalks out triumphantly.* PODBURY *places himself in a position from which he can command a view of the Musik-saal, over the top of "über Land und Meer," and awaits results.*

CHAPTER XI.

Courtship according to Mr. Ruskin.

SCENE—*A Balcony outside the Musik-Saal of the Insel Hotel, Constance.* MISS PRENDERGAST *is seated;* CULCHARD *is leaning against the railing close by. It is about nine; the moon has risen, big and yellow, behind the mountains at the further end of the Lake; small black boats are shooting in and out of her track upon the water; the beat of the steamers' paddles is heard as they come into harbour.* CULCHARD *has just proposed.*

MISS PRENDERGAST (*after a silence*). I have already felt very strongly with Ruskin, that no girl should have the cruelty to refuse a proposal——

CULCH. (*with alacrity*). Ruskin is always so right. And—er—where there is such complete sympathy in tastes and ideas, as I venture to think exists in our own case, the cruelty would——

MISS P. Pray allow me to finish! "Refuse a proposal *at once*" is Ruskin's expression. He also says (if my memory does not betray me), that "no lover should have the insolence to think of being accepted at once." You will find the passage somewhere in *Fors*.

CULCH. (*whose jaw has visibly fallen*). I cannot say I recall it at this moment. Does he hold that a lover should expect to be accepted by—er —instalments, because, if so——

MISS P. I think I can quote his exact words. "If she simply doesn't like him, she may send him away for seven years——"

CULCH. (*stiffly*). No doubt that course is open to her. But why seven, and where is he expected to go?

Courtship according to Mr. Ruskin.

MISS P. (*continuing calmly*). "He vowing to live on cresses and wear sackcloth meanwhile, or the like penance."

CULCH. I feel bound to state at once that, in my own case, my position at Somerset House would render anything of that sort utterly impracticable.

MISS P. Wait, please,—you are so impetuous. "If she likes him a little,"—(CULCHARD'S *brow relaxes*)—"or thinks she might come to like him in time, she may let him stay near her,"—(CULCHARD *makes a movement of relief and gratitude*)—"putting him always on sharp trial, and requiring, figuratively, as many lion-skins or giants' heads as she thinks herself worth."

CULCH. (*grimly*). "Figuratively" is a distinct concession on Ruskin's part. Still, I should be glad to know——

MISS P. If you will have a little more patience, I will make myself clear. I have always determined that when the—ah—occasion presented itself, I would deal with it on Ruskinian principles. I propose in your case—presuming of course that you are willing to be under vow for me—to adopt a middle course.

CULCH. You are extremely good. And what precise form of—er—penance did you think of?

MISS P. The trial I impose is, that you leave Constance to-morrow—with Mr. Podbury.

CULCH. (*firmly*). If you expect me to travel for seven years with him, permit me to mention that I simply cannot do it. My leave expires in three weeks.

MISS P. I mentioned no term, I believe. Long before three weeks are over we shall meet again, and I shall be able to see how you have borne the test. I wish you to correct, if possible, a certain intolerance in your attitude towards Mr. Podbury. Do you accept this probation, or not?

CULCH. I—ah—suppose I have no choice. But you really must allow me to say that it is *not* precisely the reception I anticipated. Still, in your service, I am willing to endure even Podbury—for a strictly limited period; that I *do* stipulate for.

Miss P. That, as I have already said, is quite understood. Now go and arrange with Mr. Podbury.

Culch. (*to himself, as he retires*). It is *most* unsatisfactory; but at least Podbury is disposed of!

The same Scene, a quarter of an hour later. Podbury *and* Miss Prendergast.

Podb. (*with a very long face*). No, I *say*, though! Ruskin doesn't say all that?

Miss P. I am not in the habit of misquoting. If you wish to verify the quotation, however, I dare say I could find you the reference in *Fors Clavigera*.

Podb. (*ruefully*). Thanks—I won't trouble you. Only it does seem rather rough on fellows, don't you know. If every one went on his plan—well, there wouldn't be many marriages! Still, I never thought you'd say "Yes" right off. It's like my cheek, I know, to ask you at all; you're so awfully clever and that. And if there's a chance for me, I'm game for anything in the way of a trial. Don't make it stiffer than you can help, that's all!

Miss P. All I ask of you is to leave me for a short time, and go and travel with Mr. Culchard again.

Podb. Oh, I say, Miss Prendergast, you know. Make it something else. *Do!*

Miss P. That is the task I require, and I can accept no other. It is nothing, after all, but what you came out here to do.

Podb. I didn't know him *then*, you see. And what made me agree to come away with him at all is beyond me. It was all Hughie Rose's doing —he said we should get on together like blazes. So we have—*very* like blazes!

Miss P. Never mind that. Are you willing to accept the trial or not?

Podb. If you only knew what he's like when he's nasty, you'd let me off—you would, really. But there, to please you, I'll do it. I'll stand him as long as ever I can—'pon my honour I will. Only you'll make it up to me afterwards, won't you now?

Courtship according to Mr. Ruskin. 63

Miss P. I will make no promises—a true knight should expect no reward for his service, Mr. Podbury.

Podb. (*blankly*). Shouldn't he? I'm a little new to the business,

"IT DOES SEEM RATHER ROUGH ON FELLOWS, DON'T YOU KNOW."

you see, and it *does* strike me——but never mind. When am I to trot him off?

Miss P. As soon as you can induce him to go—to-morrow, if possible.

Podb. I don't believe he'll *go*, you know, for one thing!

Miss. P. (*demurely*). I think you will find him open to persuasion. But go and try, Mr. Podbury.

Podb. (*to himself, as he withdraws*). Well, I've let myself in for a nice thing! Rummest way of treating a proposal *I* ever heard of. I should just like to tell that fellow Ruskin what I think of his precious ideas. But there's *one* thing, though—she can't care about Culchard, or she wouldn't want him carted off like this. . . . Hooray, I never thought of that before! Why, there he is, dodging about to find out how *I've* got on. I'll tackle him straight off.

[Culchard *and* Podbury *meet at the head of the staircase, and speak at the same moment.*

Culch. Er—Podbury, it has occurred to me that we might——

Podb. I say, Culchard, we really ought to——

} leave this place to-morrow!

Podb. Hullo! we're both of one mind for once, eh? (*To himself.*) Poor old beggar! Got the sack! That explains a lot. Well, I won't tell him anything about this business just now.

Culch. So it appears. (*To himself.*) Had his *quietus*, evidently. Ah, well, I won't exult over him.

[*They go off together to consult a time-table.*

Miss P. (*on the balcony musing*). Poor fellows! I couldn't very well say anything more definite at present. By the time I see them again, I may understand my own heart better. Really, it is rather an exciting sensation, having two suitors under vow and doing penance at the same time—and all for my sake! I hope, though, they won't mention it to one another—or to Bob. Bob does not understand these things, and he might ——But after all, there are only *two* of them. And Ruskin distinctly says that every girl who is worth *anything* ought always to have half a dozen or so. Two is really *quite* moderate.

CHAPTER XII.

Culchard descends from the Clouds.

SCENE—*In front of the Hôtel Bodenhaus at Splügen. The Diligence for Bellinzona is having its team attached. An elderly Englishwoman is sitting on her trunk, trying to run through the last hundred pages of a novel from the Hotel Library before her departure.* PODBURY *is in the Hotel, negotiating for sandwiches.* CULCHARD *is practising his Italian upon a very dingy gentleman in smoked spectacles, with a shawl round his throat.*

THE DINGY ITALIAN (*suddenly discovering* CULCHARD'S *nationality*). Ecco, siete Inglese! Lat us spika Ingelis. I onnerstan' 'im to ze bottomside. (*Laboriously, to* CULCHARD, *who tries to conceal his chagrin.*) 'Ow menni time you employ to go since Coire at here? (C. *nods with vague encouragement.*) Vich manners of vezzer you vere possess troo your travels—mosh ommerella? (C.'s *eyes grow vacant.*) Ha, I *tink* it vood! Zis day ze vicket root sall 'ave plenti 'orse to pull, &c., &c. (*Here* PODBURY *comes up, and puts some rugs in the coupé of the diligence.*) You sit at ze beginning-end, hey? better, you tink, zan ze mizzle? I too, zen, sall ride at ze front—we vill spika Ingelis, altro!

PODB. (*overhearing this, with horror*). One minute, Culchard. (*He draws him aside.*) I say, for goodness' sake, don't let's have that old organ-grinding Johnny in the *coupé* with *us!*

CULCH. Organ-grinder! you are so *very* insular! For anything you can tell, he may be a decayed nobleman.

PODB. (*coarsely*). Well, let him decay somewhere else, that's all! Just

IN THE BERNARDINO PASS, DURING THE ASCENT.

CULCH. Glorious view one gets at each fresh turn of the road, Podbury! Look at Hinter-rhein, far down below there, like a toy village,

AN ELDERLY ENGLISHWOMAN IS SITTING ON HER TRUNK.

and that vast desolate valley, with the grey river rushing through it, and the green glacier at the end, and these awful snow-covered peaks all round—*look*, man!

Culchard Descends from the Clouds.

PODB. I'm looking, old chap. It's all there, right enough!

CULCH. (*vexed*). It doesn't seem to be making any particular impression on you, I must say!

PODB. It's making me deuced peckish, I know that—how about lunch, eh!

CULCH. (*pained*). We are going through scenery like this, and all you think of is—lunch! (PODBURY *opens a basket.*) You may give me one of those sandwiches. What made you get *veal?* and the bread's all crust, too! Thanks, I'll take some claret.... (*They lunch; the vehicle meanwhile toils up to the head of the Pass.*) Dear me, we're at the top already! These rocks shut out the valley altogether—much colder at this height, eh? Don't you find this keen air most exhilarating?

PODB. (*shivering*). Oh very, do you mind putting your window up? Thanks. You seem uncommon chirpy to-day. Beginning to get *over* it, eh?

CULCH. We shan't get over it for some hours yet.

PODB. I didn't mean the Pass, I meant—(*hesitating*)—well, your little affair with Miss Prendergast, you know.

CULCH. My little affair? Get over? (*He suddenly understands.*) Oh, ah, to be sure. Yes, thank you, my dear fellow, it is not making me *particularly* unhappy. [*He goes into a fit of silent laughter.*

PODB. Glad to hear it. (*To himself.*) 'Jove, if he only knew what *I* know! [*He chuckles.*

CULCH. *You* don't appear to be exactly heartbroken?

PODB. I? why *should* I be—about *what?*

CULCH. (*with an affectation of reserve*). Exactly, I was forgetting. (*To himself.*) It's really rather humorous. (*He laughs again.*) Ha, we're beginning to go down now. Hey for Italy—la bella Italia! (*The diligence takes the first curve.*) Good Heavens, what a turn! We're going at rather a sharp pace for downhill, eh? I suppose these Swiss drivers know what they're about, though.

PODB. Oh, yes, generally—when they're not drunk. I can only see this fellow's boots—but they look to me a trifle squiffy.

CULCH. (*inspecting them, anxiously*). He does seem to drive very recklessly. *Look* at those leaders—heading right for the precipice. . . . Ah, just saved it! How we do lurch in swinging round!

Podb. Topheavy—I expect, too much luggage on board—have another sandwich?

Culch. Not for me, thanks. I say, I wonder if it's safe, having no parapet, only these stone posts, eh?

Podb. Safe enough—unless the wheel catches one—it was as near as a toucher just then—aren't you going to smoke? No? *I* am. By the way, what were you so amused about just now, eh?

Culch. *Was* I amused? (*The vehicle gives another tremendous lurch.*) Really, this is *too* horrible!

Podb. (*with secret enjoyment.*) We're right enough, if the horses don't happen to stumble. That off-leader isn't over sure-footed—did you see *that*? (Culch. *shudders.*) But what's the joke about Miss Prendergast?

Culch. (*irritably*). Oh, for Heaven's sake, don't bother about that *now!* I've something else to think about. My goodness, we were nearly over that time! What are you looking at?

Podb. (*who has been leaning forward*). Only one of the traces—they've done it up with a penny ball of string, but I dare say it will stand the strain. You aren't *half* enjoying the view, old fellow.

Culch. Yes, I am. Magnificent!—glorious!—isn't it?

Podb. Find you see it better with your eyes shut? But I say, I wish you'd explain what you were sniggering at.

Culch. Take my advice, and don't press me, my dear fellow; you may regret it if you do!

Podb. I'll risk it. It must be a devilish funny joke to tickle you like that. Come, out with it!

Culch. Well, if you must know, I was laughing. . . . Oh, he'll *never* get those horses round in. . . . I was—er—rather amused by your evident assumption that I must have been *rejected* by Miss Prendergast.

Podb. Oh, was *that* it? And you're nothing of the kind, eh?

[*He chuckles again.*

Culch. (*with dignity*). No doubt you will find it very singular; but,

Culchard Descends from the Clouds. 69

as a matter of fact, she—well, she most certainly did not *discourage* my pretensions.

PODB. The deuce she didn't! Did she tell you Ruskin's ideas about courtship being a probation, and ask you if you were ready to be under vow for her, by any chance?

CULCH. This is too bad, Podbury! you must have been there, or you couldn't possibly know!

PODB. Much obliged, I'm sure. I don't listen behind doors, as a general thing. I suppose, now, she set you a trial of some kind, to prove your mettle, eh? [*With another chuckle.*

CULCH. (*furiously*). Take care—or I may tell you more than you bargain for!

PODB. Go on—never mind *me*. Bless you, *I'm* under vow for her too, my dear boy. Fact!

CULCH. That's impossible, and I can prove it. The service she demanded was, that I should leave Constance at once—with you. Do you understand—with *you*, Podbury!

PODB. (*with a prolonged whistle*). My aunt!

CULCH. (*severely*). You may invoke every female relative you possess in the world, but it won't alter the fact, and that alone ought to convince you——

PODB. Hold on a bit. Wait till you've heard *my* penance. She told me to cart *you* off. *Now*, then!

CULCH. (*faintly*). If I thought she'd been trifling with us both like that, I'd never——

PODB. She's no end of a clever girl, you know. And, after all, she may only have wanted time to make up her mind.

CULCH. (*violently*). I tell you *what* she is—she's a cold-blooded pedantic prig, and a systematic flirt! I loathe and detest a prig, but a flirt I despise—yes, *despise*, Podbury!

PODB. (*with only apparent irrelevance*). The same to you, and many of 'em, old chap! Hullo, we're going to stop at this inn. Let's get out and stretch our legs and have some coffee.

[*They do; on returning, they find the* ITALIAN GENTLEMAN *smiling blandly at them from inside the coupé.*

The It. G. Goodaby, dear frens, a riverderla! I success at your chairs. I vish you a pleasure's delay!

Podb. But I say, look here, Sir, we're going on, and you've got our place!

The It. G. Sank you verri moch. I 'ope so.

[*He blows* Podbury *a kiss.*

Podb. (*with intense disgust*). How on earth are we going to get that beggar out? Set the Conductor at him, Culchard, do—you can talk the lingo best!

Culch. (*who has had enough of* Podbury *for the present*). Talk to him yourself, my dear fellow, *I*'m not going to make a row. [*He gets in.*

Podb. (*to* Conductor). Hi! sprechen sie Französisch, oder was? *il-y-a quelque chose dans mon siège, dites-lui de*—what the deuce is the French for "clear out"?

Cond. *Montez, Monsieur, nous bartons, montez vîte alors !*

[*He thrusts* Podbury, *protesting vainly, into the intérieur, with two peasants, a priest, and the elderly Englishwoman. The diligence starts again.*

CHAPTER XIII.

On revient Toujours!

SCENE—*A hundred yards or so from the top of Monte Generoso, above Lake Lugano.* CULCHARD, *who, with a crowd of other excursionists, has made the ascent by rail, is toiling up the steep and very slippery slope to the summit.*

CULCH. (*to himself, as he stops to pant*). *More* climbing! I thought this line was supposed to go to the top! But that's Italian all over—hem—as Podbury would say! Wonder, by the way, if he expected to be asked to come with me. I've no reason for sacrificing myself like that any longer! (*He sighs.*) Ah, Hypatia, if you could know what a dreary disenchanted blank you have made of my life! And I who believed you capable of appreciating such devotion as mine!

A VOICE BEHIND. My! If I don't know that back I'll just give up! How've *you* been getting along all this time, Mr. Culchard?

CULCH. (*turning*). Miss Trotter! A most delightful and—er—unexpected meeting, indeed!

MISS TROTTER. Well, we came up on the cars in front of yours. We've taken rooms at the hotel up here. Poppa reckoned the air would be kind of fresher on the top of this mountain, and I don't believe but what he's right either. I guess I shall want another hairpin through *my* hat. And are you still going around with Mr. Podbury? As inseparable as ever, I presume?

CULCH. Er—*about* as inseparable. That is, we are still travelling together—only, on this particular afternoon——

Miss T. He went and got mislaid? I see. He used to stray considerable over in Germany, didn't he? Well, I'm real pleased to see *you* anyway. And how's the poetry been panning out? I hope you've had a pretty good yield of sonnets?

Culch. (*to himself*). She's really grown distinctly prettier. She might show a little more *feeling*, though, considering we were almost, if not quite——(*Aloud.*) So you remember my poor poems? I'm afraid I have not been very—er—prolific of late.

Miss T. You don't say! I should think you'd have had one to show for every day, with the date to it, like a new-laid egg.

Culch. Birds don't lay—er—I mean they don't *sing*, in the dark. My light has been—er—lacking of late.

Miss T. If that's intended for me, you ought to begin chirping right away. But you're not going to tell me you've been "lounjun round en sufferin'" like—wasn't it *Uncle Remus's* Brer Terrapin? (*Catching* C.'s *look of bewilderment.*) What, don't you know *Uncle Remus?*

Culch. (*politely*). Mr. Trotter is the only relation of yours I have had the pleasure of meeting, as yet.

Miss T. Why, I reckoned *Uncle Remus* was pretty most everybody's relation by now. He's a book. But likely you've no use for our national humorous literature?

Culch. I—er—must confess I seldom waste time over the humorous literature of *any* nation.

Miss T. I guess that accounts for your gaiety! There, don't you mind *me*, Mr. Culchard. But suppose we hurry along and inspect this panorama they talk so much of; it isn't going to be any side-show. It's just a real representative mass-meeting of Swiss mountains, with every prominent peak in the country on the platform, and a deputation down below from the leading Italian lakes. It's ever so elegant,—and there's Poppa around on the top too.

On Revient Toujours. 73

On the top. Tourists discovered making more or less appropriate remarks.

FIRST TOURIST (*struggling with a long printed panorama, which flaps*

STRUGGLING WITH A LONG PRINTED PANORAMA.

like a sail). Grand view, Sir, get 'em all from here, you see! Monte Rosa, Matterhorn, Breithorn— —
  [*Works through them all conscientiously, until, much to everybody's relief, his panorama escapes into space.*
SECOND T. (*a lady, with the air of a person making a discovery*). How wonderfully small everything looks down below!
THIRD T. (*a British Matron, with a talent for incongruity*). Yes, dear,

very—*quite* worth coming all this way for; but as I was telling you, we've always been accustomed to such an evangelical service, so that our new Rector is really *rather*—but we're quite *friendly* of course; go there for tennis, and he dines with us, and all that. Still, I *do* think, when it comes to having lighted candles in broad *daylight*——(*&c., &c.*)

FOURTH T. (*an equally incongruous American*). Wa'al, yes, they show up well, cert'nly, those peaks do. But I was about to remark, Sir, I went to that particular establishment on Fleet Street. I called for a chop. And when it came, I don't deny I felt disappointed, for the plate all around was just as *dry*—! But the moment I struck a fork into that chop, Sir,—well, the way the gravy just came *gushing* out was—there, it ain't no use me trying to put it in words! But from that instant, Sir, I kinder realized the peculiar charm of your British chop.

FIFTH T. (*a discontented Teuton*). I exbected more as zis. It is nod glear enough—nod at all. Zey dolt me from ze dop you see Milan. I look all aroundt. Novere I see Milan! And I lief my obera-glass behint me in ze drain, and I slib on ze grass and sbrain my mittle finger, and altogedder I do not vish I had com.

MISS T. (*presenting* CULCHARD *to* MR. CYRUS K. T.). I guess you've met *this* gentleman before!

MR. T. Well now, that's so. I didn't just reckon I'd meet him again all this way above the sea-level though, but I'm just as pleased to see him. Rode up on the cars, I presume, Sir? Tolerable hilly road all the way, *ain't* it now? There cann't anybody say we hain't made the most of *our* time since you left us. Took a run over to Berlin; had two hours and a haff in that city, and I dunno as I keered about making a more pro-tracted visit. Went right through to Vi-enna, saw round Vi-enna. I did want, being so near, to just waltz into Turkey and see that. But I guess Turkey 'll have to keep till next time. Then back again into Switzerland, for I do seem to have kinder taken a fancy to Switzerland. I'd like to have put in more time there, and we stayed best part of a week too! But Italy's an interesting place. Yes, I'm getting considerable interested in Italy, so far as I've got. There's Geneva now——

MISS T. You do beat anything for mixing up places, Father. And you don't want to be letting yourself loose on Mr. Culchard this way. You'd better go and bring Mr. Van Boodeler along; he's round somewhere.

MR. T. I do like slinging off when I meet a friend; but I'll shut down, Maud, I'll shut down.

MISS T. Oh, there you are, Charley! Come right here, and be introduced to Mr. Culchard. He's a vurry intelligent man. My cousin, Mr. Charles Van Boodeler,—Mr. Culchard. Mr. Van Boodeler's intelligent too. He's going to write our great National Amurrcan novel, soon as ever he has time for it. That's so, isn't it?

MR. V. B. (*a slim, pale young man, with a cosmopolitan air and a languid drawl*). It's our most pressing national need, Sir, and I have long cherished the intention of supplying it. I am collecting material, and, when the psychological moment arrives, I shall write that novel. And I believe it will be a big thing, a very big thing; I mean to make it a complete compendium of every phase of our great and complicated civilization from State to State and from shore to shore. [CULCHARD *bows vaguely.*

MISS T. Yes, and the great Amurrcan public are going to rise up in their millions and boom it. Only I don't believe they'd better start booming just yet, till there's something more than covers to that novel. And how you're going to collect material for an Amurrcan novel, flying round Europe, just beats *me!*

MR. V. B. (*with superiority*). Because you don't realize that it's precisely in Europe that I find my best American types. Our citizens show up better against a European background,—it excites and stimulates their nationality, so to speak. And again, with a big subject like mine, you want to step back to get the proper focus. Now I'm *stepping* back.

MISS T. I guess it's more like skipping, Charley. But so long as you're having a good time! And here's Mr. Culchard will fix you up some sonnets for headings to the chapters. You needn't begin *right* away, Mr. Culchard; I guess there's no hurry. But we get talking and *talking*, and never look at anything. I don't call it encouraging the scenery, and that's a fact!

MR. T. (*later, to* CULCHARD). And you're pretty comfortable at your hotel? Well, I dunno, after all, what there is to keep *us* here. I guess we'll go down again and stop at Lugano, eh, Maud?

[CULCHARD *eagerly awaits her reply.*

MISS T. I declare! After bringing all my trunks way up here! But I'd just as soon move down as not; they're not unpacked any. (*Joy of* C.) Seems a pity, too, after engaging rooms here. And they looked real nice. Mr. Culchard, don't you and Mr. Podbury want to come up here and take them? They've a perfectly splendid view, and then we could have yours, you know! (C. *cannot conceal his chagrin at this suggestion.*) Well, see here, Poppa, we'll go along and try if we can't square the hotel-clerk and get our baggage on the cars again, and then we'll see just how we feel about it. I'm purrfectly indifferent either way.

CULCH. (*to himself, as he follows*). Can she be really as indifferent as she seems? I'm afraid she has very little heart! But if only she can be induced to go back to Lugano. . . . She will be at the same hotel—a great point! I wish that fellow Van Boodeler wasn't coming too, though. . . . Not that they've settled to come at all yet! . . . Still, I fancy she likes the idea. . . . She'll come—if I don't appear too anxious about it!

[*He walks on, trying to whistle carelessly.*

CHAPTER XIV.

Miss Banquo.

SCENE—*Gardens belonging to the Hôtel du Parc, Lugano. Time, afternoon; the orchestra is tuning up in a kiosk.* CULCHARD *is seated on a bench in the shade, keeping an anxious eye upon the opposite door.*

CULCH. (*to himself*). She said she had a headache, and made her father and Van Boodeler go out on the lake without her. But she certainly gave me to understand that she might come out when the band played, if she felt better. The question is, whether she *means* to feel better or not. She is the most tantalizing girl! *I* don't know what to make of her. Not a single reference, as yet, to that last talk we had at Bingen. I must see if I can't recall it to her memory—if she comes. I'll wait here, on the chance of it—we are not likely to be dis——. Confound it all—Podbury! (*with suppressed irritation as* PODBURY *comes up*). Well, do you *want* anything in particular?

PODB. (*cheerfully, as he sits down*). Only the pleasure of your society, old chap. How nicely you do put things!

CULCH. The—er—fact is, I can't promise to be a particularly lively companion just now.

PODB. Not by way of a change? Ah, well, it's a pity—but I must put up with you as you are, I suppose. You see—(*with a grin*)—I've got that vow to work out.

CULCH. Possibly—but *I* haven't. As I've already told you—I retire.

PODB. Wobbled back to Miss Trotter again, eh? Matter of taste, of course, but, for my part, I think your *first* impression of her was nearer the truth—she's not what I call a highly cultivated sort of girl, y' know.

CULCH. You are naturally exacting on that point, but have the goodness to leave my first impressions alone, and—er—frankly, Podbury, I see no necessity (*now*, at all events) to take that ridiculous—hum—penance *too* literally. We are *travelling* together, and I imagine that is enough for Miss Prendergast.

PODB. It's enough for *me*—especially when you make yourself so doosid amiable as this. You needn't alarm yourself—you won't have any more of my company than I can help; only I *must* say, for two fellows who came out to do a tour *together*, it's——

[*Walks away, grumbling.*

Later. The band has finished playing; MISS TROTTER *is on the bench with* CULCHARD.

MISS T. And you mean to tell me you've never met anybody since you even cared to converse with?

CULCH. (*diplomatically*). Does that strike you as so very incredible?

MISS T. Well, it strikes me as just a *little* too thin. I judged you'd go away, and forget I ever existed.

CULCH. (*with tender reproach*). How little you know me! I may not be an—er—demonstrative man, my—er—feelings are not easily roused, but, once roused, well—(*wounded*)—I think I may claim to possess an ordinary degree of constancy!

MISS T. Well, I'm sure I *ought* to feel it a vurry high compliment to have you going round grieving all this time on *my* account.

CULCH. Grieving! Ah, if I could only *tell* you what I went through! (*Decides, on reflection, that the less he says about this the better.*) But all that is past. And now may I not expect a more definite answer to the question I asked at Bingen? Your reply then was—well, a little ambiguous.

MISS T. I guess it's got to be just about as ambiguous now—there don't seem anything I *can* say. There's times when I feel as if it might be sort of elevating and improving to have you shining around; and there's other times when I suspect that, if it went on for any considerable

Miss Banquo.

period, likely I'd weaken. I'm not just sure. And I cann't ever make myself believe but what you're disapproving of me, inside of you, most all the time!

CULCH. Pray dismiss such—er—morbid misgivings, dear Miss Trotter.

"HOW LITTLE YOU KNOW ME."

Show that you do so by accepting me as your guide and companion through life!

MISS T. My! but that sounds like a proposal?

CULCH. I intended it to bear that—er—construction. It *is* a proposal —made after the fullest reflection.

MISS T. I'm ever so obliged. But we don't fix things quite that way in my country. We want to feel pretty sure, first, we shann't get left. And it don't seem to me as if I'd had opportunities enough of studying your leading characteristics. I'll have to study them some more before I know whereabouts I am; and I want you to understand that I'm not going to commit myself to anything at present. That mayn't be sentiment, but I guess it's common-sense, anyway. And all *you*'ve got to do is, just to keep around, and kind of impress me with a conviction that you're the vurry brightest and best man in the entire universe, and I don't believe you'll find much difficulty about *that*. And now I guess we'll go into *table d'hôte*—I'm just as *ravenous!*

CULCH. (*to himself, as he follows her*). Really, this is not much better than Ruskin, after all. But I don't despair. That last remark was distinctly encouraging!

SCENE.—*A large Salle à Manger, decorated in the Pompeian style. Table d'hôte has begun.* CULCHARD *is seated between* MISS TROTTER *and a large and conversational stranger. Opposite are three empty chairs.*

CULCHARD'S NEIGHBOUR. Then you're going on to Venice? Well, you take *my* advice. When you get there, you ask for tunny. Don't forget—*tunny!*

CULCH. (*who wants to talk to* MISS T.). Tunny? Thank you. I—er —will certainly remember his name, if I require a guide.

HIS N. A guide? No, no—tunny's a *fish*, Sir, a coarse red fish, with flesh like a raw beefsteak.

CULCH. Is that so? Then I will make a point of asking for it— if I want raw beefsteak. [*Attempts to turn to* MISS T.

HIS N. That's what *I* did when I was at Venice. I sent for the Manager. He came. I said to him, "Look here, I'm an Englishman. My name's Bellerby. (CULCHARD *bows in patient boredom.*) I've heard of your Venetian tunny. I wish to taste it. *Bring* me some!"

CULCH. (*crushingly*). A most excellent method of obtaining it, no doubt. (*To* WAITER.) *Numéro vingt-sept, demi bouteille de Chianti, et siphon!*

His N. You don't wait till I've *done*, Sir! I *didn't* obtain it—not at first. The man made excuses. I was prepared for *that*. I told him plainly, "I know what *you're* thinking—it's a cheap fish, and you fancy I'm ordering it out of economy!"

Culch. (*raising his eyebrows for* Miss T.'s *benefit*). Of course, he naturally *would* think so. And *that* is how you got your tunny? I see.

[Mr. Bellerby *stares at him suspiciously, and decides to suppress the remainder of his tunny.*]

Miss T. This hotel seems to be thinning some. We've three ghosts right in front of us this evening.

Culch. (*turning with effusion*). So we have! My friend is one, and he'll be here presently, but I much prefer myself to see every seat occupied. There is something so depressing about a vacant chair, don't you think?

Miss T. It's calculated to put one in mind of *Macbeth's* little dinner-party, certainly. But you can cheer up, Mr. Culchard, here comes a couple of belated *Banquos*. My gracious, I *do* like that girl's face—she has such a perfectly lovely expression, and looks real superior too!

Culch. (*who has just dropped his glasses into his soup*). I—ah which lady are you referring to? (*He cleans and adjusts his glasses —to discover that he is face to face with* Miss Hypatia Prendergast.) Oh ... I—I see—precisely, quite so! (*He turns to* Bellerby *to cover his confusion and avoid meeting* Miss Prendergast's *eye.*) I beg your pardon, you were describing how you caught a tunny? Pray continue.

Mr. Bellerby (*stiffly*). Excuse me, I don't seem fortunate enough to have secured your undivided attention.

Culch. (*with intense interest*). Quite the contrary, I assure you! You were saying you always ordered it out of economy?

Mr. B. Pardon *me*—I was saying nothing of the sort. I was saying that I told the Manager I knew that was why he *thought* I ordered it —a rather different thing! "You're quite wrong," I said. "You may pay twopence-halfpenny a pound for it, and charge me half-a-crown, if you like, but I mean to *taste* that tunny!" I was determined not to be done out of my tunny, Sir!

CULCH. (*breathlessly*). And what did the tunny—I mean the Manager—say to *that?*

MR. B. Oh, made more difficulties—it wasn't to be got, and so on. At last I said to him (very quietly, but he saw I was in earnest), "Now I tell you what it *is*—I'm going to *have* that tunny, and, if you refuse to give it me,—well, I shall just send my courier *out* for it, that's all!" So, with *that*, they brought me some—and anything more delicious I never tasted in all my life!

CULCH. (*to himself*). If I can only keep him on at this tunny! (*Aloud.*) And—er—what *does* it taste like exactly, now?

MR. B. (*pregnantly*). You *order* it, Sir—*insist* on having it. Then you'll *know* what it tastes like! [*He devotes himself to his soup.*

CULCH. (*with his eyes lowered—to himself*). I *must* look up in another minute—and then! [*He shivers.*

CHAPTER XV.

Culchard comes out Nobly.

SCENE—*The Table d'Hôte at Lugano;* CULCHARD *has not yet caught* MISS PRENDERGAST'S *eye.*

CULCHARD (*to* MR. BELLERBY). Have you—ah—been up Monte Generoso yet?

MR. B. No. (*After reflecting.*) No, I haven't. But I was greatly struck by its remarkably bold outline from below. Indeed, I dashed off a rough sketch of it on the back of one of my visiting cards. I ought to have it somewhere about me now. (*Searching himself.*) Ah, I thought so! (*Handing a vague little scrawl to* CULCHARD, *who examines it with the deepest interest.*) I knock off quite a number of these while I'm abroad like this. Send 'em in letters to relatives at home—gives them a notion of the place. They are—ar—kind enough to value them. (CULCHARD *makes a complimentary mumble.*) Yes, I'm a very rapid sketcher. Put me with regular artists, and give us half an hour, and I—ar—venture to say I should be on terms with them. Make it *three* hours, and—well, I dare say I shouldn't be in it.

PODBURY (*who has dropped into the chair next to* MISS PRENDERGAST *and her brother*). Bob, old chap, I'll come in the middle, if you don't mind. I say, this *is* ripping—no idea of coming across you so soon as this. (*Lowering his voice, to* MISS P.) Still pegging away at my "penance," you see!

MISS PREND. The pleasure is more than mutual; but do I understand that Mr. ——? So *tiresome*, I left my glasses up in my room!

[*She peers up and down the line of faces on her own side of the table.*

84   *The Travelling Companions.*

Miss T. (*to* Culch.). I want you should notice that girl. I think she looks just as nice as she can be, don't you?

"I KNOCK OFF QUITE A NUMBER OF THESE WHILE I'M ABROAD LIKE THIS."

Culch. (*carefully looking in every other direction*). I—er—mumble—mumble—don't exactly——

[*Here a Waiter offers him a dish containing layers of soles disguised under brown sauce;* Culchard *mangles it with an ineffectual spoon. The Waiter, with pitying contempt,* "*Tut-tut-tut! Pesce, Signore—feesh!*" Culch. *eventually lands a sole in a very damaged condition.*

Podb. (*to* Miss P.). No—not this side—just opposite. (*Here* Culch., *in fingering a siphon which is remarkably stiff on the trigger, contrives to send a spray across the table and sprinkle* Miss Prendergast, *her brother, and* Podbury, *with impartial liberality*). Now don't you see him? As playful as ever, isn't he! Don't try to make out it was an accident, old fellow. Miss Prendergast knows you!

[*Misery of* Culchard.

Culchard comes out Nobly.

Miss P. (*graciously*). Pray don't apologize, Mr. Culchard; not the least harm done! You must forgive me for not recognizing you before, but you know of old how provokingly short-sighted I am, and I've forgotten my glasses.

Culch. (*indistinctly*). I—er—not at all ... most distressed, I assure you ... really no notion——

Miss T. (*in an undertone*). Say, you *know* her, then? And you never let on!

Culch. Didn't I? Oh, surely! yes, I've—er—*met* that lady. (*With grateful deference to* Mr. Bellerby, *who has just addressed him.*) You are an Art-Collector? Indeed? And—er—have you—er—?

Mr. B. I've the three finest Bodgers in the kingdom, Sir, and there's a Gubbins—a *Joe* Gubbins, mind you, not *John*—that's hanging now in the morning-room of my place in the country that I wouldn't take a thousand pounds for! I go about using my eyes and pick 'em up cheap. Cheapest picture *I* ever bought was a Prout—thirty-two by twenty; got it for two pound ten! Unfinished, of course, but it only wanted the colour being brought up to the edge. *I* did that. Took me half a day, and *now*—well, any dealer would give me hundreds for it! But I shall leave it to the nation, out of respect for Prout's memory.

Bob Pr. (*to* Podbury). Yes, came over by the St. Gothard. Who is that girl who was talking to Culchard just now? Do you know her? I say, I wish you'd introduce me some time.

Miss T. (*to* Culchard). You don't seem vurry bright this evening. I'd like you to converse with your friend opposite, so I could get a chance to chip in. I'm ever so interested in that girl!

Culch. Presently—presently, if I have an opportunity. (*Hastily to* Mr. B.) I gather that you paint yourself, Sir?

Mr. B. Well, yes. I assure you I often go to a Gallery, see a picture there that takes my fancy, go back to my office, and paint it in half an hour from memory—so like the original that, if it were framed, and hung up alongside, it would puzzle the man who painted it to know t'other from which! I have indeed! I paint original pictures, too. Most important thing I ever did was—let me see now—three feet by two and three-quarters. I was most successful in getting an effect of rose-coloured snow against the sky. I sponged it up, and —well, it came right somehow. *Luck*, that was, not skill, you know. I sent that picture to the Royal Academy, and they did me the honour to—ar—reject it.

CULCH. (*vaguely*). An—er—honour, indeed.—(*In despair, as* MR. B. *rises.*)—You—— You're not *going!*

MR. B. (*consolingly*). Only into the garden, for coffee. I observe you are interested in Art. We will—ar—resume this conversation later.

[*Rises;* MISS PRENDERGAST *rises too, and goes towards the garden.*

CULCH. (*as he follows, hastily*). I must get this business over—if I can. But I wish I knew exactly *how* much to tell her. It's really very awkward—between the two of them. I'm afraid I've been a little too precipitate.

IN THE GARDEN; A FEW MINUTES LATER.

MISS PREND. (*who has retired to fetch her glasses—with gracious playfulness*). Well, Mr. Culchard, and how has my knight performed his lady's behests?

CULCH. May I ask *which* knight you refer to?

MISS P. (*slightly changing countenance*). Which! Then—you know there is another? Surely there is nothing in that circumstance to— to offend—or hurt you?

CULCH. Offended? (*Considers whether this would be a good line to take.*) Hardly *that.* Hurt? Well, I confess to being pained—very much pained, to discover that I was unconsciously pitted—against Podbury!

MISS P. But why? I have expressed no preference as yet. You can scarcely have become so attached to him that you dread the result of a successful rivalry!

CULCH. (*to himself*). It's a loop-hole—I'll try it. (*Aloud.*) You have divined my feeling exactly. In—er—obeying your commands, I have learned to know Podbury better—to see in him a sterling nature, more worthy, in some respects, than my own. And I know how deeply

Culchard comes out Nobly.

he has centred all his hopes upon you, Miss Prendergast. Knowing, seeing that as I—er—*do*, I feel that—whatever it costs me—I cannot run the risk of wrecking the—er—life's happiness of so good a fellow. So you must really allow me to renounce vows accepted under—er—an imperfect comprehension of the—er—facts! [*Wipes his brow.*

MISS P. This is quite too Quixotic. Reflect, Mr. Culchard. Is such a sacrifice demanded of you? I assure you I am perfectly neutral at present. I *might* prefer Mr. Podbury. I *really* don't know. And—and I don't *like* losing one of my suitors like this!

CULCH. Don't tempt me! I—I mustn't listen, I cannot. No, I renounce. Be kind to Podbury—try to recognize the good in him ... he is so devoted to you—make him happy, if you can!

MISS P. (*affected*). I—I really can't tell you how touched I am, Mr. Culchard. I can guess what this renunciation must have cost you. It—it gives me a better opinion of human nature ... it does, indeed!

CULCH. (*loftily, as she rises to go in*). Ah, Miss Prendergast, *don't* lose your faith in human nature! Trust me, it is—er—full of surprises! (*Alone.*) Now am I an abominable humbug, or what? I swear I felt every word I said, at the time. Curious psychological state to be in. But I'm out of what might have been a very unpleasant mess, at all events!

MISS T. (*coming upon him from round a corner*). Well, I'm *sure*, Mr. Culchard!

CULCH. You are a young lady of naturally strong convictions, I am aware. But what are you so sure of at the present moment?

MISS T. Well, I guess I'm not just as sure of *you* as I should like to be, anyway. Seems to me, considering you've been so vurry inconsolable away from me, you'd a good deal to say to that young lady in the patent folders. And I'd like an explanation—you're right down splendid at explaining most things.

CULCH. (*with virtuous indignation*). So you actually suspect me of having carried on a flirtation!

MISS T. I guess girls don't use their pocket-handkerchiefs that way over the weather. Who *is* she, anyway?

Culch. (*calmly*). If you insist on knowing, she is the lady to whom Mr. Podbury has every prospect of being engaged. I hope your mind is at ease *now?*

Miss T. Well, I expect my mind would have stood the strain as it was—so it's Mr. Podbury who's her admirer? See here, you're going to introduce me to that girl right away. It's real romantic, and I'm perfectly dying to make her acquaintance!

Culch. Hum—well. She is—er—*peculiar*, don't you know, and I rather doubt whether you will have much in common.

Miss T. Well, if you don't introduce me, I shall introduce myself, that's all.

Culch. By all means. (*To himself.*) Not if *I* can prevent it, though!

CHAPTER XVI.

Culchard feels slightly Uncomfortable.

SCENE—*Terrace and Grounds of the Grand Hôtel Villa d'Este, on Lake Como.* PODBURY *and* CULCHARD *are walking up and down together.*

PODB. Well, old chap, your resigning like that has made all the difference to *me*, I can tell you!

CULCH. If I have succeeded in advancing your cause with Miss Prendergast, I am all the better pleased, of course.

PODB. You have, and no mistake. She's regularly taken me in hand, don't you know—she says I've no intelligent appreciation of Italian Art; and gad, I believe she's right there! But I'm pulling up—bound to teach you a lot, seeing all the old altar-pieces I do! And she gives me the right tips, don't you see; she's no end of a clever girl, so well-read and all that! But I say—about Miss Trotter? Don't want to be inquisitive, you know, but you don't seem to be much *about* with her.

CULCH. I—er—the feelings I entertain towards Miss Trotter have suffered no change—quite the reverse, only—and I wish to impress this upon you, Podbury—it is undesirable, for—er—many reasons, to make my attentions—er—too conspicuous. I—I trust you have not alluded to the matter to—well, to Miss Prendergast, for example?

PODB. Not I, old fellow—got other things to talk about. But I don't quite see why——

CULCH. You are not *required* to see. I don't *wish* it, that is all. I—er—think that should be sufficient.

PODB. Oh, all right, *I'll* keep dark. But she's bound to know sooner or later, now she and Miss Trotter have struck up such a friendship. And Hypatia will be awfully pleased about it—why *shouldn't* she, you know? . . . I'm going to see if there's any one on the tennis-court, and get a game if I can. Ta-ta!

CULCH. (*alone*). Podbury knows very little about women. If Hyp—Miss Prendergast—once found out *why* I renounced my suitorship, I should have very little peace, I know that—I've taken particular care not to betray my attachment to Maud. I'm afraid she's beginning to notice it,

"BOUND TO TEACH YOU A LOT, SEEING ALL THE OLD ALTAR-PIECES I DO!"

but I must be careful. I don't like this sudden intimacy between them—it makes things so very awkward. They've been sitting under that tree over there for the last half-hour, and goodness only knows what confidences they may have exchanged! I really must go up and put a stop to it, presently.

UNDER THE TREE.

HYPATIA. I only tell you all this, dearest, because I *do* think you have rather too low an opinion of men as a class, and I wanted to show you that I have met at least *one* man who was capable of a real and disinterested devotion.

MAUD. Well, I allowed that was about your idea.

HYP. And don't you recognize that it was very fine of him to give up everything for his friend's sake?

MAUD. I guess it depends how much "everything" amounted to.

HYP. (*annoyed*). I thought, darling, I had made it perfectly plain what a sacrifice it meant to him. *I* know how much he—I needn't tell you there are certain symptoms one can*not* be deceived in.

MAUD. No, I guess you needn't tell me *that*, love. And it was perfectly lovely of him to give you up, when he was under vow for you and all, sooner than stand in his friend's light—only I don't just see how that was going to help his friend any.

HYP. Don't you really? Not when the friend was under vow for me too?

MAUD. Well, Hypatia Prendergast! And how many admirers do you have around under vow, as a regular thing?

HYP. There were only those two. Ruskin permits as many as seven at one time.

MAUD. That's a vurry liberal allowance, too. I don't see how there'd be sufficient suitors to go round. But maybe each gentleman can be under vow for seven distinct girls, to make things sort of square now?

HYP. Certainly not. The whole beauty of the idea lies in the unselfish and exclusive devotion of every knight to the same sovereign lady. In this case I happen to know that the—a—individual had never met his ideal until—

MAUD. Until he met you? At Nuremberg, wasn't it? My! And what was his name? Do tell!

HYP. You must not press me, dear Maud, for I cannot tell that—even to you.

MAUD. I don't believe but what I could guess. But say, you didn't care any for *him*, or you'd never have let him go like that? *I* wouldn't. I should have suspected there was something behind!

HYP. My feelings towards him were purely potential. I did him the simple justice to believe that his self-abnegation was sincere. But, with your practical, cynical little mind, darling, you are hardly capable of— excuse me for saying so—of appreciating the real value and meaning of such magnanimity!

MAUD. Oh, I guess I *am*, though. Why, here's Mr. Culchard coming along. Well, Mr. Culchard?

CULCH. I—ah—appear to have interrupted a highly interesting conversation?

MAUD. Well, we were having a little discussion, and I guess you're in time to give the casting vote—Hypatia, you want to keep just where you are, do you hear? I mean you should listen to Mr. Culchard's opinion.

CULCH. (*flattered*). Which I shall be delighted to give, if you will put me in possession of the—er—facts.

MAUD. Well, these are the—er—facts. There were two gentlemen under vow—maybe you'll understand the working of that arrangement better than I do?—under vow for the same young lady. [Hypatia Prendergast, sit still, or I declare I'll pinch you!] One of them comes up and tells her that he's arrived at the conclusion the other admirer is the better man, and, being a friend of his, he ought to retire in his favour, and he does it, too, right away. Now *I* say that isn't natural —he'd some other motive. Miss Prendergast here will have it he was one of those noble unselfish natures that deserve they should be stuffed for a dime museum. What's *your* opinion now?

CULCH. (*perspiring freely*). Why—er—really, on so delicate a matter, I—I—— [*He maunders.*

HYP. Maud, why *will* you be so headstrong! (*In a rapid whisper.*) Can't you see . . . can't you *guess*? . . .

MAUD. I guess I want to make sure Mr. Culchard isn't that kind of magnanimous man himself. I shouldn't want him to renounce *me!*

HYP. Maud! You might at *least* wait until Mr. Culchard has——

Culchard feels slightly Uncomfortable.

MAUD. Oh, but he *did*—weeks ago, at Bingen. And at Lugano, too, the other day, he spoke out tolerable plain. I guess he didn't wish any secret made about it—*did* you, Mr. Culchard?

CULCH. I—ah—this conversation is rather ... If you'll excuse me—— [*Escapes with as much dignity as he can command.*

MAUD. Well, my dear,—that's the sort of self-denying hairpin *he* is! What do you think of him *now*?

HYP. I do not think so highly of him, I confess. His renunciation was evidently less prompted by consideration for his friend than by a recollection—tardy enough, I am afraid—of the duty which bound him to *you*, dearest. But if you had seen and heard him, as I did, you would not have doubted the *reality* of the sacrifice, whatever the true reason may have been. For myself, I am conscious of neither anger nor sorrow—my heart, as I told you, was never really affected. But what must it be to *you*, darling!

MAUD. Well, I believe I'm more amused than anything.

HYP. Amused! But surely you don't mean to have anything more to do with him?

MAUD. My dear girl, I intend to have considerable more to do with him before I'm through. He's under vow for *me* now, anyway, and I don't mean he should forget it, either. He's my monkey, and he's got to jump around pretty lively, at the end of a tolerable short chain, too. And I guess, if it comes to renouncing, all the magnanimity's going to be on *my* side this time!

IN AN AVENUE.

CULCH. (*to himself, as he walks hurriedly on*). I only just saved myself in time. I don't *think* Maud noticed anything—she couldn't have been so innocent and indifferent if she had. ... And Hypatia won't enlighten her any further now—after what she knows. It's rather a relief that she *does* know. ... She took it very well, poor girl—*very* well. I expect she is really beginning to put up with Podbury—I'm sure I *hope* so, sincerely!

CHAPTER XVII.

Culchard cannot be "Happy with Either."

SCENE—*Under the Colonnade of the Hôtel Grande Bretagne, Bellagio.* CULCHARD *is sitting by one of the pillars, engaged in constructing a sonnet. On a neighbouring seat a group of smart people are talking over their acquaintances, and near them is another visitor, a* MR. CRAWLEY STRUTT, *who is watching his opportunity to strike into the conversation.*

MRS. HURLINGHAM. Well, she'll *be* Lady Chesepare some day, when anything happens to the old Earl. He was looking quite ghastly when we were down at Skympings last. But they're frightfully badly off *now*, poor dears! Lady Driblett lets them have her house in Park Lane for parties and that—but it's wonderful how they live at all!

COLONEL SANDOWN. He looked pretty fit at the Rag the other day. Come across the Senlacs anywhere? Thought Lady Senlac was going abroad this year.

MR. CRAWLEY STRUTT. Hem—I saw it mentioned in the *Penny Patrician* that her Ladyship had——

MRS. HURL. (*without taking the slightest notice of him*). She's just been marryin' her daughter, you know—rather a good match, too. Not what I call pretty,—smart-lookin', that's all. But then her *sister* wasn't pretty till she married.

COL. SAND. Nice family she married into! Met her father-in-law, old Lord Bletherham, the other morning, at a chemist's in Piccadilly—he'd dropped in there for a pick-me-up; and there he was, tellin' the chemist all the troubles he'd had with his other sons marryin' the way they did,

Culchard cannot be Happy with Either. 95

and that. Rum man to go and confide in his chemist, but he's like that—fond of the vine!

Mr. C. S. Er—her—it's becoming a very serious thing, Sir, the way our aristocracy is deteriorating, is it not?

"I DON'T KNOW IF YOU'RE ACQUAINTED WITH A PAPER CALLED THE 'PENNY PATRICIAN'?"

Col. S. Is it? What have they been up to now, eh? I haven't seen a paper for days.

Mr. C. S. I mean these mixed marriages, and, well, their general goings on. I don't know if you're acquainted with a paper called the

Penny Patrician? I take it in regularly, and I assure *you*—loyal supporter of our old hereditary institutions as I am—some of the revelations I read about in high life make me blush—yes, downright *blush* for them!

[MRS. HURLINGHAM *retires.*

COL. S. Do they, though? If I were you I should let 'em do their own blushin', and save my pennies.

MR. C. S. (*deferentially*). No doubt you're right, Sir, but I *like* the *Patrician* myself—it's very smartly written. Talking of that, do you happen to know the ins and outs of that marriage of young Lord Goslington's? Something very mysterious about the party he's going to marry—who *are* her people now?

COL. S. Can't say, I'm sure—no business of mine, you know.

MR. C. S. There I venture to think you're wrong, Sir. It's the business of everybody—the *duty*, I may say—to see that the best blood of the nation is not——(COL. S. *turns into the hotel;* MR. C. S. *sits down near* CULCH.)—Remarkably superior set of visitors staying here, Sir! My chief objection to travel always is, that it brings you in contact with parties you wouldn't think of associating with at home. I was making that same remark to a very pleasant little fellow I met on the steamer—er—Lord Uppersole, I think it was—and he entirely concurred. Your friend made us acquainted.—(PODBURY *comes out of the hotel.*)—Ah, here *is* your friend, —(*To* PODB.)—Seen his Lordship about lately, Sir?—Lord Uppersole I *mean*, of course!

PODB. Uppersole? No—he's over at Cadenabbia, I believe.

MR. C. S. A highly agreeable spot to stay at. Indeed, I've some idea myself of—— Exceedingly pleasant person his Lordship—so affable, so completely the gentleman!

PODB. Oh, he's affable enough—for a boot-maker. I always give him a title when I see him, for the joke of the thing—he likes it.

MR. C. S. *He* may, Sir. I consider a title is not a thing to be treated in that light manner. It—it was an unpardonable liberty to force me into the society of that class of person—unpardonable, Sir!

[*He goes.*

PODB. Didn't take much *forcing*, after he once heard me call him

Culchard cannot be Happy with Either. 97

"Lord Uppersole"! Where are all the others, eh? Thought we were going up to the Villa Serbelloni this afternoon.

CULCH. I—er—have not been consulted. Are they—er—*all* going? [*With a shade of anxiety.*

PODB. I believe so. You needn't be afraid, you know. Hypatia won't have the chance of ragging you now—she and Miss Trotter have had a bit of a breeze.

CULCH. I rather gathered as much. I think I could guess the——

PODB. Yes, Hypatia's rather uneasy about poor old Bob; thinks Miss Trotter is—well, carrying on, you know. She is no end of a little flirt—*you* know that well enough!—(C. *disclaims impatiently.*) Here you all are, eh?—(*To* MISS P., MISS T., *and* BOB.)—Well, who knows the way up to the villa?

MISS T. It's through the town, and up some steps by the church—you can't miss it. But Mr. Prendergast is going to show me a short cut up behind the hotel—aren't you, Mr. Prendergast?

MISS P. (*icily*). I really think, dear, it would be better if we all kept together—for so *many* reasons!

CULCH. (*with alacrity*). I agree with Miss Prendergast. A short cut is invariably the most indirect route.

MISS P. (*with intention*). You hear what Mr. Culchard says, my dear Maud? He advocates direct ways, as best in the long run.

MISS T. It's only going to be a short run, my love. But I'm vurry glad to observe that you and Mr. Culchard are so perfectly harmonious, as I'm leaving him on your hands for a spell. Aren't you ever coming, Mr. Prendergast? [*She leads him off, a not unwilling captive.*

A PATH IN THE GROUNDS OF THE VILLA SERBELLONI.

PODB. (*considerately, to* CULCHARD, *who is following* MISS PRENDER-GAST *and him, in acute misery*). Look here, old fellow, Miss Prendergast would like to sit down, I know; so don't you bother about keeping with us if you'd rather *not*, you know! [CULCHARD *murmurs an inarticulate protest.*

O

Miss P. Surely, Mr. Podbury, you are aware by this time that Mr. Culchard has a perfect mania for self-sacrifice!
  [CULCHARD *drops behind, crushed.*

AMONG THE RUINS AT THE TOP OF THE HILL.

CULCH. (*who has managed to overtake* MISS T. *and her companion*). Now *do* oblige me by looking through that gap in the pines towards Lecco. I particularly wish you to observe the effect of light on those cliffs—it's well worth your while.

MISS T. Why, certainly, it's a view that does you infinite credit. Oh, you *didn't* take any hand in the arrangement? But ain't you afraid if you go around patting the scenery on the head this way, you'll have the lake overflow?

BOB P. Ha-ha-ha! One in the eye for *you*, Culchard!

CULCH. (*with dignity*). Surely one may express a natural enthusiasm without laying oneself open —— ?

MISS T. Gracious, yes! I should hope you wouldn't want to show your enthusiasm *that* way—like a Japanese nobleman!

CULCH. (*to himself*). Now that's coarse—*really* coarse!—(*Aloud.*)— I seem to be unable to open my mouth now without some ridiculous distortion——

MISS T. My!—but that's a serious symptom—isn't it? You don't feel like you were going to have lock-jaw, do you, Mr. Culchard?

  [CULCHARD *falls back to the rear once more. Later*—MR. VAN
    BOODELER *has joined the party;* HYPATIA *has contrived to
    detach her brother.* CULCHARD *has sought refuge with*
    PODBURY.

MISS T. (*to* VAN B.). So that's what kept you? Well, it sounds just too enchanting. But I cann't answer for what Miss Prendergast will say to it. It mayn't suit her notions of propriety.

MR. VAN B. I expect she'll be superior to Britannic prejudices of that kind. I consider your friend a highly cultivated and charming lady, Maud. She produces that impression upon me.

Culchard cannot be Happy with Either.

MISS T. I presume, from that, she has shown an intelligent interest in the great Amurrcan novel?

MR. VAN B. Why, yes; it enlists her literary sympathies—she sees all its possibilities.

MISS T. And they're pretty numerous, too. But here she comes. You'd better tell her your plan right now.

MISS P. (*in an earnest undertone to* BOB, *as they approach, followed by* CULCH. *and* POD.). You *must* try and be sensible about it, Bob; if *you* are too blind to see that she is only——

BOB (*sulkily*). All *right!* Haven't I *said* I'd go? What's the good of *jawing* about it?

MR. V. B. (*to* MISS P.). I've been telling my cousin I've been organising a little water-party for this evening—moonlight, mandolins, Menaggio. If you find the alliteration has any attractions, I hope you and your brother will do me the pleasure of——

MISS P. I'm afraid not, thanks. We have all our packing to do. We find we shall have to leave early to-morrow.

[VAN B.'s *face falls ;* BOB *listens gloomily to* MISS T.'s *rather perfunctory expressions of regret ;* PODBURY *looks anxious and undecided ;* CULCHARD *does his best to control an unseemly joy.*

CHAPTER XVIII.

A Suspension of Hostilities.

SCENE—*The roof of Milan Cathedral; the innumerable statues and fretted pinnacles show in dazzling relief against the intense blue sky. Through the open-work of the parapet is seen the vast Piazza, with its yellow toy tram cars, and the small crawling figures which cast inordinately long shadows. All around is a maze of pale-brown roofs, and beyond, the green plain blending on the horizon with dove-coloured clouds in a quivering violet haze.* CULCHARD *is sitting by a small doorway at the foot of a flight of steps leading to the Spire.*

CULCHARD (*meditating*). I think Maud must have seen from the tone in which I said I preferred to remain below, that I object to that cousin of hers perpetually coming about with us as he does. She's far too indulgent to him—a posing, affected prig, always talking about the wonderful things he's *going* to write! He had the impudence to tell me I didn't know the most elementary laws of the sonnet this morning! Withering repartee seems to have no effect whatever on him. I wish I had some of Podbury's faculty for flippant chaff! I wonder if he and the Prendergasts really are at Milan. I certainly thought I recognised—— If they are, it's very bad taste of them, after the pointed way in which they left Bellagio. I only hope we shan't——

> [*Here the figure of* MISS PRENDERGAST *suddenly emerges from the door;* CULCHARD *rises and stands aside to let her pass; she returns his salutation distantly, and passes on with her chin in the air; her brother follows, with a side-jerk of recognition.* PODBURY *comes last, and halts undecidedly.*

A Suspension of Hostilities.

PODB. (*with a rather awkward laugh*). Here we are again, eh? (*Looks after* MISS P., *hesitates, and finally sits down by* CULCHARD.) Where's the fascinating Miss Trotter? How do you come to be off duty like this?

SHE PASSES ON WITH HER CHIN IN THE AIR.

CULCH. (*stiffly*). The fascinating Miss Trotter is up above with Van Boodeler, so my services are not required.

PODB. Up above? And Hypatia just gone up with Bob! Whew, there'll be ructions presently! Well out of it, you and I! So it's Boodeler's turn now? That's rough on *you*—after Hypatia had whistled poor old Bob off. As much out in the cold as ever, eh?

CULCH. I am nothing of the kind. I find him distasteful to me, and avoid him as much as I can, that's all. I wish, Podbury, er—I *almost* wish you could have stayed with me, instead of allowing the Prendergasts to carry you off as they did. You would have kept Van Boodeler in order.

PODB. Much obliged, old chap; but I'm otherwise engaged. Being kept in order myself. Oh, I *like* it, you know. She's developing my mind like winking. Spent the whole morning at the Brera, mugging up these old Italian Johnnies. They really are clinkers, you know. Raphael, eh?—and Giotto, and Mantegna, and all that lot. As Hypatia says, for intensity of—er—religious feeling, and—and subtlety of symbolism, and—and so on, they simply take the cake—romp in, and the rest nowhere! I'm getting quite the connoisseur, I can tell you!

CULCH. Evidently. I suppose there's no chance of a—a *reconciliation* up there? [*With some alarm.*

PODB. Don't you be afraid. When Hypatia once gets her quills up, they don't subside so easily! Hallo! isn't this old Trotter?

[*That gentleman appears in the doorway.*

MR. T. Why, Mr. Podbury, so you've come along here? That's *right!* And how do you like Milan? I like the place first-rate—it's a live city, Sir. And I like this old cathedral, too; it's well constructed—they've laid out money on it. I call it real ornamental, all these little figgers they've stuck around—and not two of 'em a pair either. Now, they might have had 'em all alike, and no one any the wiser up so high as this; but it certainly gives it more variety, too, having them different. Well, I'm going up as high as ever I *can* go. You two better come along up with me.

ON THE TOP.

MISS P. (*as she perceives* MISS T. *and her companion*). Now, Bob, pray remember all I've told you! [BOB *turns away, petulantly.*

MISS T. (*aside, to* VAN B.). I guess the air's got cooler up here,

A Suspension of Hostilities.

Charley. But if that girl imagines she's going to freeze *me!* (*Advancing to* Miss P.) Why, my dear, it's almost too sweet for anything, meeting you again!

Miss P. You're extremely kind, Maud; I wish I could return the compliment; but really, after what took place at Bellagio, I——

Miss T. (*taking her arm*). Well, I'll own up to being pretty horrid—and so were you; but there don't seem any sense in our meeting up here like a couple of strange cats on tiles. I won't fly out any more, there! I'm just dying for a reconciliation; and so is Mr. Van Boodeler. The trouble I've had to console that man! He never met anybody before half so interested in the great Amurrcan Novel. And he's wearying for another talk. So you'd better give that hatchet a handsome funeral, and come along and take pity on him.

[Hyp., *after a struggle, yields, half-reluctantly, and allows herself to be taken across to* Mr. Van B., *who greets her effusively.* Miss T. *leaves them together.*

Bob P. (*who has been prudently keeping in the background till now, decides that his chance has come*). How do you do, Miss Trotter? It's awfully jolly to meet you again like this!

Miss T. Well, I guess that remark would have been more convincing if you'd made it a few minutes earlier.

Bob. I—I—you see, I didn't know ... I was afraid—I rather thought——

Miss T. You don't get much further with *rather* thinking, as a general rule, than if you didn't think at all. But if you're at all anxious to run away the way you did at Bellagio, you needn't be afraid *I'll* hinder you.

Bob. (*earnestly*). Run away! *Do* you think I'd have gone if—I've felt dull enough ever since, without *that!*

Miss T. Oh, I expect you've had a beautiful time. *We* have.

Miss P. (*coming up*). Robert, I thought you wanted to see the Alps? You should come over to the other side, and——

Miss T. I'll undertake that he sees the Alps, my dear, presently—when we're through our talk.

Miss P. As you please, dear. But (*pointedly*) did I not see Mr. Culchard below?

Miss T. You don't mean to say you're wearied of Mr. Van Boodeler *already!* Well, Mr. Culchard will be along soon, and I'll loan him to you. I'll tell him you're vurry anxious to converse with him some more. He's just coming along now, with Mr. Podbury and Poppa.

Miss P. (*under her breath*). Maud! if you *dare*——!

Miss T. Don't you *dare* me, then—or you'll see. But I don't want to be mean unless I'm obliged to.

[Mr. Trotter, *followed by* Culchard *and* Podbury, *arrives at the upper platform.* Culchard *and* Podbury *efface themselves as much as possible.* Mr. Trotter *greets* Miss Prendergast *heartily.*

Mr. T. Well now, I call this sociable, meeting all together again like this. I don't see why in the land we didn't *keep* together. I've been saying so to my darter here, ever since Bellagio—ain't that so, Maud? And *she* didn't know just how it came about either.

Miss P. (*hurriedly*). We—we had to be getting on. And I am afraid we must say good-bye now, Mr. Trotter. I want Bob and Mr. Podbury to see the Da Vinci fresco, you know, before the light goes. (Bob *mutters a highly disrespectful wish concerning that work of Art.*) We *may* see you again, before we leave for Verona.

Mr. T. Verona? Well, I don't care if I see Verona myself. Seems a pity to separate now we *have* met, *don't* it? See here, now, we'll *all* go along to Verona together—how's that, Maud? Start whenever *you* feel like it, Miss Prendergast. How does that proposal strike you? I'll be real hurt if you cann't take to my idea.

Miss T. The fact is, Poppa, Hypatia isn't just sure that Mr. Prendergast wouldn't object.

Bob P. I—object? Not *much!* Just what I should *like*, seeing Verona with—all *together*, you know!

Miss T. Then I guess *that's* fixed. (*Aside, to* Miss P., *who is speechless.*) Come, you haven't the heart to go and disappoint my poor Cousin Charley by saying you won't go! I expect he'll be perfectly enchanted

A Suspension of Hostilities.

to be under vow—unless you've filled up *all* the vacancies already! (*Aloud, to* VAN B., *as he approaches.*) We've persuaded Miss Prendergast to join our party. I hope you feel equal to entertaining her?

VAN B. I shall be proud to be permitted to try. (*To* MISS P.) Then I may take it that you agree with me that the function of the future American fictionist will be—— [*They move away conversing.*

PODB. (*to* CULCH.). I say, old fellow, we're to be travelling companions again, after all. And a jolly good thing, too, *I* think!... eh?

CULCH. Oh, h'm—quite so. That is—but no doubt it will be an advantage—(*with a glance at* VAN B., *who is absorbed in* MISS P.'S *conversation*)—in—er—*some* respects. (*To himself.*) Hardly from poor dear Podbury's point of view, I'm afraid though! However, if *he* sees nothing——! [*He shrugs his shoulders, pityingly.*

CHAPTER XIX.

Crumpled Roseleaves.

SCENE—*The Tombs of the* SCALIGERS *at Verona. A seedy and voluble Cicerone, who has insisted upon volunteering his services, is accompanying* MISS TROTTER, BOB PRENDERGAST, *and* CULCHARD. *It is a warm afternoon, and* CULCHARD, *who has been intrusted with* MISS T.'S *recent purchases—two Italian blankets, and a huge pot of hammered copper—is not in the most amiable of moods.*

THE CICERONE (*in polyglot*). Ecco, Signore (*pointing out the interlaced ladders in the wrought-iron railings*), l'échelle, la scala, c'est tout flexible—(*He shakes the trellis*)—molto, molto curioso!

CULCH. (*bitterly, to the other two*). I *warned* you how it would be! We shall have this sort of thing all the afternoon *now!*

MISS T. Well, I don't mind; he's real polite and obliging—and that's something, anyway!

CULCH. Polite and obliging! Now I *ask* you—has he given us the slightest atom of valuable information *yet?*

MISS T. I guess he's too full of tact to wish to interfere with your special department.

THE CIC. (*to* CULCHARD, *who looks another way*). Ici le tombeau di Giovanni della Scala, Signore. Verri grazioso, molto magnifique, joli conservé! (*He skips up on the pedestal, and touches a sarcophagus.*) Non bronzo—verde-antique! [*Nods at* CULCHARD, *with a beaming smile.*

CULCH. (*with a growl*). Va bene, va bene—*we* know all about it!

BOB P. *You* may; but you might give Miss Trotter and me a chance, you know!

THE CIC. Zees, Marmor di Carrara; sat, Marmor di Verona—Verona marbre. Martino Primo a fait bâtir. (*Counting on his fingers for* CULCHARD'S *benefit.*) Quattuor dichième secolo- *fotteen!*

"BELLISSIMO SCULTORE!"

CULCH. Will you kindly understand that I am quite capable of estimating the precise period of this sculpture for myself.

THE CIC. Si-sì, Signore. Scultore Bonino da Campiglione. (*With a wriggle of deferential enthusiasm.*) Bellissimo scultore!

Miss T. He's got an idea you find him vurry instructive, Mr. Culchard, and I guess, if you want to disabuse him, you'd better do it in Italian.

Culch. I think my Italian is equal to conveying an impression that I can willingly dispense with his society. (*To the* Cic.) Andate via—do you understand? An-da-te *via!*

The Cic. (*hurt, and surprised*). Ah, Signore!

[*He breaks into a fervent vindication of his value as guide, philosopher, and friend.*

Miss T. I guess he's endeavouring to intimate that his wounded self-respect isn't going to be healed under haff a dollar. And every red cent I had went on that old pot! Mr. Culchard, will you give him a couple of francs for me?

Culch. I—er—really see no necessity. He's done nothing whatever to deserve it!

Bob P. (*eagerly*). May *I*, Miss Trotter? (*Producing a ten-lire note.*) This is the smallest change I've got.

Miss T. No, I guess ten francs would start him with more self-respect than he's got any use for. Mr. Culchard will give him three—that's one apiece—to punish him for being so real mean!

Culch. (*indignantly*). Mean? because I——! (*He pays and dismisses the* Cic.) Now we can examine these monuments in peace—they are really—er—unique examples of the sepulchral pomp of Italian mediævalism.

Miss T. They're handsome tombs enough—but considerable cramped. I should have thought these old Scallywags would have looked around for a roomier burying lot. (*To* Culchard, *who shivers.*) You aren't feeling sick any?

Culch. No—only pained by such a travesty of a noble name. "Scallywags" for Scaligers seems to me, if I may say so, a very cheap form of humour!

Miss T. Well, it's more than cheap—it isn't going to cost you a cent, so I should think you'd appreciate it!

Bob P. Haw—score for *you*, Miss Trotter!

Culch. I should have thought myself that mere personality is hardly

enough to give point to any repartee—there is a slight difference between brilliancy and—er—*brutality!*
BOB P. Hullo! You and I are being sat upon pretty heavily, Miss Trotter.
MISS T. I guess our Schoolmaster's abroad. But why Mr. Culchard should want to make himself a train out of my coverlets, I don't just see—he looks majestic enough without that.
[CULCHARD *catches up a blanket which is trailing, and says bad words under his breath.*

AT THE TOMB OF JULIET.

CULCH. (*who is gradually recovering his equanimity*). Think of it! the actual spot on which *Romeo* and *Juliet*—Shakspeare's *Juliet*—drew their last breath! Does it not realise the tragedy for you?
MISS T. Well, no—it's a disappointing tomb. I reckoned it would look less like a horse-trough. I should have expected *Juliet's* Poppa and Momma would want, considering all the facts of the case, to throw more style into her monument!
CULCH. (*languidly*). May not its very simplicity—er—attest the sincerity of their remorse?
MISS T. Do you attach any particular meaning to that observation now? (CULCHARD *bites his lip.*) I notice this tomb is full of visiting cards—my! but ain't that curious?
CULCH. (*instructively*). It only shows that this place is not without its pathos and interest for *most* visitors, no matter what their nationality may be. You don't feel inclined yourself to——?
MISS T. To leave a pasteboard? Why I shouldn't sleep any all night, for fear she'd return my call!
CULCH. (*producing a note-book*). It's fanciful, perhaps—but, if you don't mind waiting a little, I should like to contribute—not my card, but a sonnet. I feel one on its way.
BOB P. Better make sure the tomb's *genuine* first, hadn't you? Some say it *isn't*.

CULCH. (*exasperated*). I *knew* you'd make some matter-of-fact remark of that kind! There—it's no use! Let us go.

MISS T. Why, your sonnets seem as skeery as those lizards there! I hope Juliet won't ever know what she's missed. But likely you'll mail those verses on to her later. [*She and* BOB P. *pass on, laughing.*

CULCH. (*following*). She only affects this vulgar flippancy to torment me. If I didn't know *that*—— There, I've left that infernal pot behind now! [*Goes back for it, wrathfully.*

In the Amphitheatre ; MISS PRENDERGAST, PODBURY, *and* VAN BOODELER, *are seated on an upper tier.*

PODB. (*meditatively*). I suppose they charged highest for the lowest seats. Wonder whether a lion ever nipped up and helped himself to some fat old buffer in the Stalls when the martyrs turned out a leaner lot than usual!

VAN B. There's an ingenuous modernity about our friend's historical speculations that is highly refreshing.

MISS P. There is, indeed—though he might have spared himself and *us* the trouble of them if he had only remembered that the *podium* was invariably protected by a railing, and occasionally by *euripi*, or trenches, You surely learnt that at school, Mr. Podbury?

PODB. I—I dare say. Forgotten all I learnt at school, you know!

VAN B. I should infer now, from that statement, that you enjoyed the advantages of a pretty liberal education?

PODB. If that's meant to be cutting, I should save it up for that novel of yours; it may seem smart—*there!*

MISS P. Really, Mr. Podbury, if you choose to resent a playful remark in that manner, you had better go away.

PODB. Perhaps I had. (*Rises, and moves off huffily.*) D—— his playfulness! 'Pon my word, poor old Culchard was *nothing* to that beggar! And she backs him up! But there—it's all part of my probation! (*Here* CULCHARD *suddenly appears, laden with burdens.*) Hullo! are you *moving*, or what?

Crumpled Roseleaves.

CULCH. I am merely carrying a few things for Miss Trotter. (*Drops the copper pot, which bounds down into the arena.*) Dash the thing! . . . (*Returning with it.*) It's natural that, in my position, I should have these —er—privileges. (*He trips over a blanket.*) Conf——Have you happened to see Miss Trotter about, by the way?

PODB. Fancy I saw her down below just now—with Bob. I expect they're walking round under the arches.

CULCH. Just so. Do you know, Podbury, I almost think I'll go down and find her. I—I'm curious to hear what her impressions of a place like this are. Such a scene, you know,—so full of associations with—er—the splendours and cruelties of a corrupt past—must produce a powerful effect upon the fresh untutored mind of an American girl, eh?

MISS T.'S *voice* (*distinctly from arena*). I'd like ever so much to see Buffalo Bill run his Show in here—he'd just make this old circus hum!

MISS P.'S *voice* (*indistinctly from topmost tier*). Almost fancy it all . . . Senators—*equites—populus—pullati* . . . yellow sunlight striking down through *vellarium* . . . crimsoned sand . . . *mirmillo* fleeing before *secutor* . . . Diocletian himself, perhaps, lolling over there on *cubiculum* . . . &c. &c. &c.

CULCH. The place appears to excite Miss Prendergast's enthusiasm, at all events! [*Sighs.*

PODB. Rath-er! But then she's no end of a classical swell, you know! [*Sighs.*

CULCH. (*putting his arm through* PODBURY'S). Ah, well, my dear Podbury, one mustn't expect too much, must one?

PODB. I *don't*, old chap—only I'm afraid *she* does. Suppose we toddle back to the hotel, eh? Getting near *table d'hôte* time.

[*They go out arm-in-arm.*

CHAPTER XX.

Put not your Faith in 'Fibibus.'

SCENE—*The interior of a covered gondola, which is conveying* CULCHARD *and* PODBURY *from the Railway Station to the Hotel Dandolo, Venice. The gondola is gliding with a gentle sidelong heave under shadowy bridges of stone and cast-iron, round sharp corners, and past mysterious blank walls, and old scroll-work gateways, which look ghostly in the moonlight.*

CULCH. (*looking out of the felze window, and quoting conscientiously*).

"I saw from out the wave her structures rise,
As from the stroke of the enchanter's wand."

PODB. For rest, see guide-books, *passim*, eh? Hanged if *I* can see any structures with this thing on, though! Let's have it off, eh? (*He crawls out and addresses* GONDOLIER *across the top.*) Hi! *Otez-moi ceci. entendez-vous?* (*Drums on roof of felze with fists; the* GONDOLIER *replies in a torrent of Italian.*) Now a London cabby would see what I wanted at once. This chap's a fool!

CULCH. He probably imagines you are merely expressing your satisfaction with Venice. And I don't see how you expect him to remove the entire cabin here! (PODBURY *crawls in again, knocking his head.*) I think we did well to let the—the others travel on first. More *dignified*, you know!

PODB. Um—don't see any particular dignity in missing the train, myself!

CULCH. They won't know it was not intentional. And I think,

Put not your Faith in 'Fidibus.' 113

Podbury, we should go on—er—asserting ourselves a little while by holding rather aloof. It will show them that we don't mean to put up with——

"HI! OTTZ-MOI CECI!"

Podb. Don't see that either. Not going to let that beast, Van Boodeler, have it *all* his own way!

Culch. Surely you know he decided suddenly to stay at Vicenza? He said so at breakfast. But I will *not* have your friend Bob perpetually——

Q

Podb. At breakfast? Oh, I came down late. Vicenza, eh? Then *he's* out of it! Hooray! But as for Bob, *he's* all right too. Oh, I forgot you cut *déjeuner*. Hypatia had another squabble with Miss Trotter, and poor old Bob got dragged into it as usual, and now they ain't on speaking terms.

Culch. (*overjoyed*). You don't say so! Then all *I* can say, Podbury, is that if we two can't manage, in a place like this, to recover all the ground we have lost——

Podb. More water than ground in a place like this, eh? But *I* know what you mean—we *must* be duffers if we don't leave Venice engaged men —which we're not as yet, worse luck!

Culch. No—but we *shall* be, if we only insist upon being treated seriously.

Podb. She treats me a devilish deal *too* seriously, my boy. But there, never mind—things will go better now!

Scene—*A double-bedded room in the Grand Hotel Dandolo, which* Podbury *and* Culchard *have to share for the night.*

Podb. (*from his bed, suspiciously, to* Culchard, *who is setting fire to a small pastille in a soap-dish*). I say, old chappie, bar *fireworks*, you know! What the deuce *are* you up to over there?

Culch. Lighting a "fidibus." Splendid thing to drive out mosquitoes. (*The pastille fizzes, and begins to emit a dense white smoke, and a suffocating odour.*)

Podb. (*bounding*). Mosquitoes! It would drive a *dragon* out. Phew —ah! (Culchard *closes the window.*) You *don't* mean to say you're going to shut me up in this infernal reek on a stifling night like this?

Culch. If I didn't, the mosquitoes would come in again.

Podb. Come in? With that pastille doing the young Vesuvius! Do you think a mosquito's a born fool? (*He jumps out and opens the window.*) I'm not going to be smoked like a wasp's nest, *I* can tell you!

CULCH. (*calmly shutting it again, as* PODBURY *returns to bed*). You'll be grateful to me by-and-by.
 [*Slips between his mosquito curtains in a gingerly manner, and switches off the electric light. A silence.*
 PODB. I say, you ain't asleep, are you? Think we shall see anything of them to-morrow, eh?
 CULCH. See? I can *hear* one singing in my ear at this moment. (*Irritably.*) You *would* open the window!
 PODB. (*sleepily*). Not mosquitoes. I meant Hypatia, and the—haw—yaw—Trotters.
 CULCH. How can *I* tell? (*Second silence.*) Podbury! What did I *tell* you? One's just bitten me—the *beast!* (*He turns on the light, and slaps about frantically.*) I say, I can hear him buzzing all over the place!
 PODB. So can I hear *you* buzzing. How the dickens is a fellow to get to sleep while you're playing Punch and Judy in there?
 CULCH. He's got me on the nose now! There's a lot outside. Just turn off the light, will you? I daren't put my arm out. (*To* Mosquito.) You brute! (*To* PODB.) Podbury, *do* switch off the light—like a good fellow!
 PODB. (*dreamily*). Glass up, Gondolier . . . stifling in this cab . . . drive me . . . nearest Doge. [*He snores.*
 CULCH. Brutal selfishness! (*Turns out the light himself.*) Now if I can only get off to sleep while that little beast is quiet——
 MOSQUITO (*ironically, in his ear*). Ping-a-wing-wing!

Same Scene; the next morning.

 CULCH. (*drawing* PODBURY'S *curtains*). Here, wake up, Podbury—it's just eight. (PODBURY *sits up, and rubs his eyes.*) I've had a *horrible* night, my dear fellow! I'm stung to such an extent! But (*hopefully*) I suppose there's nothing to *show* particularly, eh?
 [*Presenting his countenance for inspection.*
 PODB. Not much of your original features, old fellow! (*He roars with laughter.*) You've got a pair of cheeks like a raised map!

CULCH. It—it's going *down*. Nothing to what it *was*, half an hour ago!

PODB. Then I'm jolly glad you didn't call me earlier, that's all!

CULCH. It does feel a little inflamed. I wonder if I could get a little —er—violet powder, or something——?

PODB. (*with a painful want of sympathy*). Violet powder! Buy a blue veil—a good thick one!

CULCH. What sort of impression *do* you suppose I should get of Venice with a blue veil on?

PODB. Can't say—but a pleasanter one than Venice will get of you *without* it. You don't mean to face the fair Miss Trotter while you're like *that*, do you?

CULCH. (*with dignity*). Most certainly I *do*. I am much mistaken in Miss Trotter if she will attach the slightest importance to a mere temporary—er—disfigurement. These swellings never do last long. *Do* they now?

PODB. Oh, not more than a month or so, I dare say, if you can keep from touching them. (*He laughs again.*) Excuse me, old chap, but I just got you in a new light. Those mosquitoes have paid you out for that pastille—by Jove, they have!

LANDING-STEPS AND ENTRANCE OF THE HOTEL. NINE A.M.

CULCH. (*coming out a little self-consciously, and finding* MR. TROTTER). Ah, good morning! What are your—er—impressions of Venice, Mr. Trotter?

MR. TROTTER (*thoughtfully*). Well, I'm considerable struck with it, Sir. There's a purrfect freshness and novelty about Vernis that's amusing to a stranger like myself. We've nothing just like this city out West. No, *Sir*. And how are—(*Becomes aware of* CULCHARD'S *appearance*.) Say, *you* don't look like your slumbers had been one unbroken ca'm, either! The mosquitoes hev been powerful active makin' alterations in you. Perseverin' and industrious insects, Sir! Me and my darter have

Put not your Faith in 'Fidibus.'

been for a loaf round before breakfast. I dunno if you've seen *her* yet, she's——

MISS T. (*coming out from behind*). Poppa, they've fixed up our breakf—(*Sees* CULCHARD, *and turns away, covering her face*). Don't you turn your head in *this* direction, Mr. Culchard, or I guess I'll expire right away!

CULCH. (*obeying, wounded*). I confess I did *not* think a few mosquito-bites would have quite such an effect upon you!

MISS T. You're vurry polite, I'm sure! But I possess a hand-mirror; and, if you cann't bear to look me in the face, you'd better keep away!

CULCH. (*takes a hasty glance, and discovers, with a shock, that she is almost as much disfigured as himself*). Oh, I—I wasn't——(*With an effort of politeness.*) Er—I hope *you* haven't been inconvenienced at all?

MISS T. Inconvenienced! With haff a dozen healthy mosquitoes springing a surprise party on me all night! I should guess *so*. (*Noticing* C.'s *face*.) But what in the land have you been about? Well, if that isn't real *tact* now! I reckoned I'd been dealt a full hand in spots; but now I've seen you, I guess there's a straight flush against me, and I can just throw up. But you don't play Poker, *do* you? Come along in, Poppa, do. [*She goes in with* MR. T.

CULCH. (*alone, disenchanted*). I could *not* have believed any amount of bites could have made such a terrible difference in her. She looks positively *plain!* I do trust they're not *permanent*, or really——!

[*He gazes meditatively down on the lapping water.*

CHAPTER XXI.

Wearing Rue with a Difference.

SCENE—*The Steps of the Hotel Dandolo, about* 11 A.M. PODBURY *is looking expectantly down the Grand Canal*, CULCHARD *is leaning upon the Balustrade.*

PODB. Yes, met Bob just now. They've gone to the Europa, but we've arranged to take a gondola together, and go about. They're to pick me up here. Ah, that looks rather like them. (*A gondola approaches, with* MISS PRENDERGAST *and* BOB; PODBURY *goes down the steps to meet them.*) How are you, Miss Prendergast? Here I *am*, you see.

MISS P. (*ignoring* C.'s *salute*). How do you do, Mr. Podbury? Surely you don't propose to go out in a gondola in *that* hat!

PODB. (*taking off a brown "pot-hat," and inspecting it*). It—it's quite decent. It was new when I came away!

BOB (*who is surly this morning*). Hang it all, Patia! Do you want him to come out in a chimney-pot? Jump in, old fellow, never mind your tile?

PODB. (*apologetically*). I had a straw once—but I sat on it. I'm awfully sorry, Miss Prendergast. Look here, shall I go and see if I can buy one?

MISS P. Not now—it doesn't signify, for once. But a round hat and a gondola are really *too* incongruous!

PODB. Are they? A lot of the Venetians seem to wear 'em. (*He steps in.*) Now what are we going to do—just potter about?

MISS P. One hardly comes to Venice to *potter!* I thought we'd go and study the Carpaccios at the Church of the Schiavoni first —they won't take us more than an hour or so; then cross to San Giorgio Maggiore, and see the Tintorets, come back and get a general idea of the exterior of St. Mark's, and spend the afternoon at the Accademia.

PODB. (*with a slight absence of heartiness*). Capital! And—er—lunch at the Academy, I suppose?

MISS P. There does not happen to be a restaurant there—we shall see what time we have. I must say *I* regard every minute of daylight spent on food here as a sinful waste.

BOB. Now just look here, Patia, if you *are* bossing this show, you needn't go cutting us off our grub! What do *you* say, Jem?

PODB. (*desperately anxious to please*). Oh, I don't know that I care about lunch myself—much. [*Their voices die away on the water.*

CULCH. (*musing*). She might have *bowed* to me!... *She* has escaped the mosquitoes... Ah, well, I doubt if she'll find those two particularly sympathetic companions! Now I *should* enjoy a day spent in that way. Why shouldn't I, as it is? I dare say Maud will——

[*Turns and sees* MR. TROTTER.

MR. T. My darter will be along presently. She's Cologning her cheeks—they've swelled up again some. I guess you want to Cologne *your* cheeks—they're dreadful lumpy. I've just been on the Pi-azza again, Sir. It's curious now the want of enterprise in these Venetians. Any one would have expected they'd have thrown a couple or so of girder bridges across the canal between this and the Ri-alto, and run an elevator up the Campanile—but this ain't what you might call a *business* city, Sir, and that's a fact. (*To* MISS T. *as she appears.*) Hello, Maud, the ice-water cool down your face any?

MISS T. Not *much*. My face just made that ice-water boil over. I don't believe I'll ever have a complexion again—it's divided up among several dozen mosquitoes, who've no use for one. But it's vurry consoling to look at *you*, Mr. Culchard, and feel there's a pair of us. Now what way do you propose we should endeavour to forget our sufferings?

CULCH. Well, we might spend the morning in St. Mark's——?

The Travelling Companions.

Miss T. The morning! Why, Poppa and I saw the entire show inside of ten minutes, before breakfast!

Culch. Ah! (*Discouraged.*) What do you say to studying the

"I GUESS YOU WANT TO COLOGNE *your* CHEEKS—THEY'RE DREADFUL LUMPY."

Vine and Fig-tree angles and the capitals of the arcades in the Ducal Palaces? I will go and fetch the *Stones of Venice*.

Miss T. I guess you can leave those old stones in peace. I don't feel like studying up anything this morning—it's as much as ever I can do not to scream aloud!

CULCH. Then shall we just drift about in a gondola all the morning, and—er—perhaps do the Academy later?

MISS T. Not any canals in this hot sun for me! I'd be just as *sick!* That gondola will keep till it's cooler.

CULCH. (*losing patience*). Then I must really leave it to you to make a suggestion!

MISS T. Well, I believe I'll have a good look round the curiosity stores. There's ever such a cunning little shop back of the Clock Tower on the Pi-azza, where I saw some brocades that were just too sweet! So I'll take Poppa along bargain-hunting. Don't *you* come if you'd rather poke around your old churches and things!

CULCH. I don't feel disposed to—er—"poke around" alone, so, if you will allow me to accompany you,——

MISS T. Oh, I'll allow you to escort me. It's handy having some one around to carry parcels. And Poppa's bound to drop the balance every time!

CULCH. (*to himself*). That's all I am to her. A beast of burden! And a whole precious morning squandered on this confounded shopping —when I might have been—ah, well! [*Follows, under protest.*

On the Grand Canal. 9 P.M. *A brilliant moonlight night; a music-barge, hung with coloured lanterns, is moving slowly up towards the Rialto, surrounded and followed by a fleet of gondolas, amongst which is one containing the* TROTTERS *and* CULCHARD. CULCHARD *has just discovered—with an embarrassment not wholly devoid of a certain excitement—that they are drawing up to a gondola occupied by the* PRENDERGASTS *and* PODBURY.

MR. TROTTER (*meditatively*). It's real romantic. That's the third deceased kitten I've seen to-night. They haven't only a two-foot tide in the Adriatic, and it stands to reason all the sewage——

[*The two gondolas are jammed close alongside.*

R

MISS P. How absolutely magical those palaces look in the moonlight! Bob, how *can* you yawn like that?

BOB. I beg your pardon, Patia, really, but we've had rather a long day of it, you know!

MR. T. Well, now, I declare I sort of recognised those voices! (*Heartily.*) Why, how are *you* getting along in Vernis? *We're* gettin' along fust-rate. Say, Maud, here's your friend alongside!

[MISS P. *presents a stony silence.*

MISS T. (*in an undertone*). I don't see how you *can* act so, Poppa,—when you know she's just as *mad* with me!

MR. T. There! Dumned if I didn't clean forget you were out! But, see here, now—why cann't we let bygones be bygones?

BOB. (*impulsively*). Just what *I* think, Mr. Trotter, and I'm sure my sister will——

MISS P. Bob, will you kindly not make the situation more awkward than it is? If I desired a reconciliation, I think I am quite capable of saying so!

MISS T. (*in confidence to the Moon*). This Ark isn't proposing to send out any old dove, either—we've no use for an olive-branch. (*To* MR. T.) That's "*Santa Lucia*" they're singing now, Poppa.

MR. T. They don't appear to me to get the twist on it they did at Bellagio!

MISS T. You mean that night Charley took us out on the Lake? Poor Charley! he'd just love to be here—he's ever so much artistic feeling!

MR. T. Well, I don't see why he couldn't have come along if he'd wanted.

MISS T. (*with a glance at her neighbour*). I presume he'd reasons enough. He's a vurry cautious man. Likely he was afraid he'd get bitten.

MISS P. (*after a swift scrutiny of* MISS T.'S *features*). Oh, Bob, remind me to get some more of that mosquito stuff. I *should* so hate to be bitten—such a *dreadful* disfigurement!

MISS T. (*to the Moon*). I declare if I don't believe I can feel some creature trying to sting me now!

Wearing Rue with a Difference.

MISS P. Some people are hardly recognisable, Bob, and they say the marks never *quite* disappear!

MISS T. Poppa, don't you wonder what Charley's doing just now? I'd like to know if he's found any one yet to feel an interest in the great Amurrcan Novel. It's curious how interested people do get in that novel, considering it's none of it written, and never will be. I guess sometimes he makes them believe he means something by it. They don't understand it's only Charley's way!

MISS P. The crush isn't quite so bad now. Mr. Podbury, if you will kindly ask your friend not to hold on to our gondola, we should probably be better able to turn. (CULCHARD, *who had fondly imagined himself undetected, takes his hand away as if it were scorched.*) Now we can get away. (*To* Gondolier.) Voltiamo, se vi piace, prestissimo!

[*The gondola turns and departs.*

MISS T. Well, I do just enjoy making that Prendergast girl perfectly wild, and that's a fact. (*Reflectively.*) And it's queer, but I like her ever so much all the time. Don't *you* think that's too fonny of me, Mr. Culchard, now? [CULCHARD *feigns a poetic abstraction.*

CHAPTER XXII.

One Man's Meat; another Man's Poison.

SCENE—*The Campo S. S. Giovanni e Paulo. Afternoon.* CULCHARD *is leaning against the pedestal of the Colleoni Statue.*

PODBURY (*who has just come out of S. Giovanni, recognising* CULCHARD). Hullo! *alone*, eh? Thought you were with Miss Trotter?

CULCHARD. So I am. That is, she is going over a metal-worker's show-room close by, and I—er—preferred the open air. But didn't you say you were going out with the—er—Prendergasts again?

PODB. So I am. She's in the Church with Bob, so I said I'd come out and keep an eye on the gondola. Nothing much to see in *there*, you know!

CULCH. (*with a weary irony*). Only the mausoleums of the Doges—Ruskin's "Street of the Tombs"—and a few trifles of that sort!

PODB. That's all. And I'm feeling a bit done, you know. Been doing the Correr Museum all the morning, and not lunched yet! So Miss Trotter's looking at ornamental metal-work? Rather fun that, eh?

CULCH. For those who enjoy it. She has only been in there an hour, so she is not likely to come back just yet. What do you say to coming into S. S. Giovanni e Paulo again, with *me*? Those tombs form a really remarkable illustration, as Ruskin points out, of the gradual decay of——

MISS TROTTER (*suddenly flutters up, followed by an attendant carrying a studded halberd, an antique gondola-hook, and two copper water-buckets—all of which are consigned to the disgusted* CULCHARD). Just hold these a spell till I come back. Thanks ever so much . . . Well, Mr. Podbury! Aren't you going to admire my purchases? They're real antique—or if

One Man's Meat; another Man's Poison.

they aren't, they'll wear all the better ... There, I believe I'll just have to run back a minute—don't you put those things in the gondola yet, Mr. Culchard, or they'll get stolen. [*She flutters off.*

CULCH. (*helplessly, as he holds the halberd, &c.*). I suppose I shall have to stay *here* now. You're not going?

PODB. (*consulting his watch*). Must. Promised old Bob I'd relieve guard in ten minutes. Ta-ta.

[*He goes; presently* BOB PRENDERGAST *lounges out of the church.*

CULCH. If I could only make a friend of *him*! (*To* BOB.) Ah, Prendergast! lovely afternoon, isn't it? Delicious breeze!

BOB (*shortly*). Can't say. Not had much of it, at present.

CULCH. You find these old churches rather oppressive, I dare say. Er—will you have a cigarette? [*Tenders case.*

BOB. Thanks; got a pipe. (*He lights it.*) Where's Miss Trotter?

CULCH. She will be here presently. By the way, my dear Prendergast, this—er—misunderstanding between your sister and her is very unfortunate.

BOB. I know that well enough. It's none of *my* doing! And *you've* no reason to complain, at all events!

CULCH. Quite so. Only, you see, we *used* to be good friends at Constance, and—er—until recently——

BOB. Used we? Of course, if you say so, it's all right. But what are you driving at exactly?

CULCH. All I am driving at is this: Couldn't we two—er—agree to effect a reconciliation between the two ladies? So much pleasanter for—er—all parties!

BOB. I dare say. But how are you going to set about it? *I* can't begin.

CULCH. Couldn't you induce your sister to lay aside her—er—prejudice against me? Then *I* could easily——

BOB. Very likely—but I *couldn't*. I never interfere in my sister's affairs, and, to tell you the honest truth, I don't feel particularly inclined to make a beginning on your account. [*Strolls away.*

CULCH. (*to himself*). What a surly boor it is! But I don't care—I'll do him a good turn, in spite of himself! (MISS T. *returns*.) Do you know, I've just been having a chat with poor young Prendergast. He seems quite cut up at being forced to side with his sister. I undertook to—er—intercede for him. Now is it quite fair, or like your—er—usual good-nature, to visit his sister's offences—whatever they are—on him? I—I only put it to you.

MISS T. Well, to think now! I guess you're about the most unselfish saint on two legs! Now some folks would have felt jealous.

CULCH. Possibly—but I cannot accuse myself of such a failing as that.

MISS T. I'd just like to hear you accuse yourself of *any* failing! I don't see however you manage to act so magnanimous and live. I told you I wanted to study your character, and I believe it isn't going to take me vurry much longer to make up my mind about *you*. You *don't* suppose I'll have any time for Mr. Prendergast after getting such a glimpse into your nature? There, help me into the gondola, and don't talk any more about it. Tell him to go to Salviate's right away.

CULCH. (*dejectedly to himself*). I've bungled it! I might have *known* I should only make matters worse!

On the Piazzetta; it is moonlight, the Campanile and dome of San Giorgio Maggiore are silhouetted sharp and black against the steel-blue sky across a sea of silver ripples. PODBURY *and* CULCHARD *are pacing slowly arm-in-arm between the two columns.*

CULCH. And so you went on to S. Giovanni in Bragora, eh? then over the Arsenal, and rowed across the lagoons to see the Armenian convent? A delightful day, my dear Podbury! I hope you—er—appreciate the inestimable privileges of—of seeing Venice so thoroughly?

PODB. Oh, of course it's very jolly. Find I get a trifle mixed afterwards, though. And, between ourselves, I wouldn't mind—now and then, you know—just dawdling about among the shops and people, as you and the Trotters do!

CULCH. That has its charm, no doubt. But don't you find Miss Prendergast a mine of information on Italian Art and History?

One Man's Meat; another Man's Poison. 127

PODB. Don't I just—rather too *deep* for me, y' know! I say, isn't Miss Trotter immense sport in the shops and that?

"I GUESS YOU'RE THE MOST UNSELFISH SAINT ON TWO LEGS!"

CULCH. She is—er—vivacious, certainly. (PODBURY *sighs*.) You seem rather dull to-night, my dear fellow?

PODB. Not dull—a trifle out of sorts, that's all. Fact is, I don't think Venice agrees with me. All this messing about down beastly back-courts and canals and in stuffy churches—it *can't* be healthy, you know! And they've *no* drainage. I only hope I haven't caught something, as it is. I've that kind of sinking feeling, and a general lowness—*She* says I lunch too heavily—but I swear it's more than that!

CULCH. Nonsense, you're well enough. And why you should feel low, with all your advantages—in Venice as you are, and in constant intercourse with a mind adorned with every feminine gift—!

PODB. Hul-lo! why, I thought you called her a pedantic prig?

CULCH. If I used such a term at all, it was in no disparaging sense. Every earnest nature presents an—er—priggish side at times. I know that even I myself have occasionally, and by people who didn't *know* me of course, been charged with priggishness.

PODB. Have you, though? But of course there's nothing of that about *her*. Only—well, it don't signify. [*He sighs.*

CULCH. Ah, Podbury, take the good the gods provide you and be content! You might be worse off, believe me!

PODB. (*discontentedly*). It's all very well for *you* to talk—with Miss Trotter all to yourself. I suppose you're regularly engaged by this time, eh?

CULCH. Not quite. There's still a—— And your probation, that's practically at an end?

PODB. I don't know. Can't make her out. She wouldn't sit on me the way she does unless she *liked* me, I suppose. But I say, it must be awf—rather jolly for you with Miss Trotter? She's got so much *go*, eh?

CULCH. You used to say she wasn't what you call cultivated.

PODB. I know I did. That's just what I like about her! At least—well, we *both* ought to think ourselves uncommonly lucky beggars, I'm sure! [*He sighs more heavily than ever.*

CULCH. You especially, my dear Podbury. In fact, I doubt if you're half grateful enough!

PODB. (*snappishly*). Yes, I am, I tell you. *I'm* not grumbling, am I?

One Man's Meat; another Man's Poison.

I know as well as you do she's miles too good for me. Haven't I *said* so? Then what the devil do you keep on nagging at me for, eh?

CULCH. I am glad you see it in that light. Aren't you a little irritable to-night?

PODB. No, I'm not. It's those filthy canals. And the way you talk—as if a girl like Miss Trotter wasn't——!

CULCH. I really can't allow you to lecture me. I am not insensible to my good-fortune—if others are. Now we'll drop the subject.

PODB. I'm willing enough to drop it. And I shall turn in now—it's late. You coming?

CULCH. Not yet. Good-night. (*To himself, as* PODBURY *departs.*) You tasteless *dolt!*

PODB. Good-night! (*To himself, as he swings off.*) Confounded patronizing *prig!*

CHAPTER XXIII.

Pearls and Pigs.

SCENE—*The Lower Hall of the Scuola di San Rocco, Venice. British Tourists discovered studying the Tintorets on the walls and ceiling by the aid of Ruskin, Hare, and Bædeker, from which they read aloud, instructively, to one another.* MISS PRENDERGAST *has brought* "*The Stones of Venice*" *for the benefit of her brother and* PODBURY. *Long self-repression has reduced* PODBURY *to that unpleasantly hysterical condition known as* "*a fit of the giggles," which, however, has hitherto escaped detection.*

MISS P. (*standing opposite* "*The Flight into Egypt," reading*). "One of the principal figures here is the Donkey." Where *is* Mr. Podbury? [*To* P., *who reappears, humbly proffering a tin focussing-case.*) Thanks, but you need not have troubled! "The Donkey ... um—um—never seen—um—um—any of the nobler animals so sublime as this quiet head of the domestic ass"—(*here* BOB *digs* PODBURY *in the ribs behind* MISS P.'s *back*)—"chiefly owing to the grand motion in the nostril, and writhing in the ears." (*A spasmodic choke from* PODBURY.) May I ask what you find so amusing?

PODB. (*crimson*). I—I *beg* your pardon—I don't know *what* I was laughing at exactly. (*Aside to* BOB.) *Will* you shut up, confound you!

A STOUT LADY (*close by, reading from Hare*). "The whole symmetry of it depending on a narrow line of light." (*Dubiously, to her Daughter.*) I don't *quite*—oh yes, I do now—that's it—where my sunshade is—" the edge of a carpenter's square, which connects those unused tools" ... h'm—can *you* make out the "unused tools," Ethel? *I* can't ... But he says—" The Ruined House is the Jewish Dispensation." Now I should never have found *that* out for myself. (*They pass to another canvas.*) "Tintoret denies himself all aid from the features ... No time allowed for watching the expression." . . . (That reminds me—what *is* the time by your bracelet, darling?) "No blood, no stabbing, or cutting . . . but an awful substitute for these in the chiaroscuro." (Ah, yes, indeed! Do you see it, love?—in the right-hand corner.) "So that our eyes"—(*comfortably*)—"seem to become blood-shot, and strained with strange horror, and deadly vision." (Not one o'clock, *really?*—and we've to meet Papa outside Florian's for lunch at one-thirty! Dear me, we mustn't stay too long over this room.)

A SOLEMN GENTLEMAN (*struggling with a troublesome cough, who is also provided with Hare, reading aloud to his wife*). "Further enhanced by—rook—rook—rook!—a largely-made—rook—ook!—farm-servant, leaning on a ork-ork—ork—ork—or—ook!—basket. Shall I—ork!— go on?

HIS WIFE. Yes, dear, do, *please!* It makes one notice things so *much* more!   [*The* SOLEMN GENTLEMAN *goes on.*

MISS P. (*as they reach the staircase*). Now just look at this Titian, Mr. Podbury! Ruskin particularly mentions it. Do note the mean and petty folds of the drapery, and compare them with those in the Tintorets in there.

PODB. (*obediently*). Yes, I will,—a—did you mean *now*—and will it take me long, because——   [MISS PRENDERGAST *sweeps on scornfully*.

PODB. (*following, with a desperate effort to be intelligent*). They don't seem to have any Fiammingoes here.

MISS P. (*freezingly, over her shoulder*). Any *what*, Mr. Podbury? Flamingoes?

PODB. (*confidently, having noted down the name at the Accademia on his shirt-cuff*). No, "Ignoto Fiammingo," don't you know. I like that chap's style—what I call thoroughly Venetian.

[*Well-informed persons in front overhear and smile.*

MISS P. (*annoyed*). That is rather strange—because "Ignoto Fiammingo" happens to be merely the Italian for "an unknown Fleming," Mr. Podbury.   [*Collapse of* PODBURY.

BOB. (*aside to* PODBURY). You great owl, you came a cropper *that* time!

[*He and* PODBURY *indulge in a subdued bear-fight up the stairs, after which they enter the Upper Hall in a state of preternatural solemnity.*

132   *The Travelling Companions.*

The Solemn G. Now what *I* want to see, my dear, is the ork—ork—angel that Ruskin thinks Tintoretto painted the day after he saw a rook—kic—kic—kic—kingfisher.

[Bob *nudges* Podbury, *who resists temptation heroically.*

A SOLEMN GENTLEMAN STRUGGLING WITH A TROUBLESOME COUGH.

Miss P. (*reading*). . . . "the fig-tree which, by a curious caprice, has golden ribs to all its leaves."—Do you see the ribs, Mr. Podbury?

Podb. (*feebly*). Y—yes. I *believe* I do. Think they grew that sort of fig-tree formerly, or is it—a—*allegorical?*

Miss P. (*receiving this query in crushing silence*). The ceiling requires

Pearls and Pigs.

careful study. Look at that oblong panel in the centre—with the fiery serpents, which Ruskin finely compares to "winged lampreys." You're not looking in the right way to see them, Mr. Podbury!

PODD. (*faintly*). I—I did see them—*all* of them, on my honour I did! But it gives me such a crick in my neck!

MISS P. Surely Tintoret is worth a crick in the neck. Did you observe "the intense delight in biting expressed in their eyes"?

BOB. (*frivolously*). *I* did, 'Patia—exactly the same look I observed last night, in a mosquito's eye.

[PODBURY *has to use his handkerchief violently.*

THE STOUT LADY. Now, Ethel, we can just spend ten minutes on the ceiling—and then we *must* go. That's evidently Jonah in the small oval (*referring to plan*). Yes, I thought so,—it *is* Jonah. Ruskin considers "the whale's tongue much too large, unless it is a kind of crimson cushion for Jonah to kneel upon." Well, why *not?*

ETHEL. A cushion, Mother? what, *inside* the whale!

THE STOUT LADY. That we are not *told*, my love—"The submissiveness of Jonah is well given"—So true—but Papa can't bear being kept waiting for his lunch—we really ought to go now. [*They go.*

THE SOLEMN G. (*reading*). "There comes up out of the mist a dark hand." Have *you* got the dark hand yet, my dear?

HIS WIFE. No, dear, only the mist. At least, there's something that *may* be a branch; or a *bird* of some sort.

THE S. G. Ha, it's full of suggestion, full of suggestion!

[*He passes on, coughing.*

MISS P. (*to* PODBURY, *who is still quivering*). Now notice the end one—"the Fall of Manna"—not *that* end; that's the "Fall of *Man*." Ruskin points out (*reading*) "A very sweet incident. Four or five sheep, instead of pasturing, turn their heads to catch the manna as it comes down" (*here* BOB *catches* PODBURY'S *eye*), "or seem to be licking it off each other's fleeces." (PODBURY *is suddenly convulsed by inexplicable and untimely mirth.*) Really, Mr. Podbury, this is *too* disgraceful!

[*She shuts the book sharply and walks away.*

OUTSIDE; BY THE LANDING STEPS.

Miss P. Bob, go on and get the gondola ready. I wish to speak to Mr. Podbury. (*To* Podbury, *after* Bob *has withdrawn.*) Mr. Podbury, I cannot tell you how disgusted and disappointed I feel at your senseless irreverence.

Podb. (*penitently*). I—I'm really most awfully sorry—but it came over me suddenly, and I simply couldn't help myself!

Miss P. That is what makes it so very hopeless—after all the pains I have taken with you! I have been beginning to fear for some time that you are incorrigible—and to-day is really the *last* straw! So it is kinder to let you know at once that you have been tried and found wanting. I have no alternative but to release you finally from your vows—I cannot allow you to remain my suitor any longer.

Podb. (*humbly*). I was always afraid I shouldn't last the course, don't you know. I did my best—but it wasn't *in* me, I suppose. It was awfully good of you to put up with me so long. And, I say, you won't mind our being friends still, will you now?

Miss P. Of course not. I shall always wish you well, Mr. Podbury—only I won't trouble you to accompany me to any more galleries!

Podb. A—thanks. I—I mean, I know I should only be in your way and all that. And—I'd better say good-bye, Miss Prendergast. You won't want me in the gondola just now, I'm sure. I can easily get another.

Miss P. Well—good-bye then, Mr. Podbury. I will explain to Bob.

[*She steps into the gondola;* Bob *raises his eyebrows in mute interrogation at* Podbury, *who shakes his head, and allows the gondola to go without him.*

Podb. (*to himself as the gondola disappears*). So *that's* over! Hanged if I don't think I'm sorry, after all. It will be beastly lonely without anybody to bully me, and she could be awfully nice when she chose. . . . Still it *is* a relief to have got rid of old Tintoret, and not to have to bother about Bellini and Cima and that lot. . . . How that beggar Culchard will crow when he hears of it! Shan't tell him anything—if I can help it. . . But the worst of getting the sack is—people are almost *bound* to spot you. . . . I think I'll be off to-morrow. I've had enough of Venice!

CHAPTER XXIV.

The Pilgrims of Love.

SCENE—*The Piazza of St. Mark at night. The roof and part of the façade gleam a greenish silver in the moonlight. The shadow of the Campanile falls, black and broad, across the huge square, which is crowded with people listening to the Military Band, and taking coffee, &c., outside the cafés.* MISS TROTTER *and* CULCHARD *are seated at one of the little tables in front of the Quadri.*

MISS T. I'd like ever so much to know why it is you're so anxious to see that Miss Prendergast and me friendly again? After she's been treating you this long while like you were a toad—and not a popular kind of toad at that!

CULCH. (*wincing*). Of course I am only too painfully aware of—of a certain distance in her manner towards me, but I should not think of allowing myself to be influenced by any—er—merely personal considerations of that sort.

MISS T. That's real noble! And I presume, now, you cann't imagine any reason why she's been treading you so flat.

CULCH. (*with a shrug*). I really haven't troubled to speculate. Who can tell how one may, quite unconsciously, give offence—even to those who are—er—comparative strangers?

MISS T. Just so. (*A pause.*) Well, Mr. Culchard, if I wanted anything to confirm my opinion of you, I guess you've given it me!

CULCH. (*internally*). It's very unfortunate that she *will* insist on idealizing me like this!

Miss T. Maybe, now, you can form a pretty good idea already what that opinion is?

Culch. (*in modest deprecation*). You give me some reason for inferring that it is far higher than I deserve.

Miss T. Well, I don't know that you've missed your guess altogether. Are you through your ice-cream yet?

Culch. Almost. (*He finishes his ice.*) It is really most refreshing.

Miss T. Then, now you're refreshed, I'll tell you what I think about you. (Culchard *resigns himself to enthusiasm.*) My opinion of you, Mr. Culchard, is that, taking you by and large, you amount to what we Amurreans describe as "a pretty mean cuss."

Culch. (*genuinely surprised*). A mean cuss? Me! Really, this unjustifiable language is *most——!*

Miss T. Well, I don't just know what your dictionary term would be for a man who goes and vows exclusive devotion to one young lady, while he's waiting for his answer from another, and keeps his head close shut to each about it. Or a man who backs out of his vows by trading off the sloppiest kind of flap-doodle about not wishing to blight the hopes of his dearest friend. Or a man who has been trying his hardest to get into the good graces again of the young lady he went back on first, so he can cut out that same dearest friend of his, and leave the girl he's haff engaged to right out in the cold. And puts it all off on the high-toned-est old sentiments, too. But I don't consider the expression, "a mean cuss," too picturesque for that particular kind of hero myself!

Culch. (*breathing hard*). Your feelings have apparently undergone a sudden change—quite recently!

Miss T. Well, no, the change dates back considerable—ever since we were at the Villa d'Este. Only, I like Mr. Podbury pretty well, and I allowed he ought to have fair play, so I concluded I'd keep you around so you shouldn't get a chance of spoiling your perfectly splendid act of self-denial—and I guess I've *kept* you around pretty much all the time.

Culch. (*bitterly*). In other words, you have behaved like a heartless coquette!

The Pilgrims of Love.

MISS T. You may put it at that if you like. Maybe it wouldn't have been just the square thing to do if you'd been a different sort of man—but you wanted to be taught that you couldn't have all the

"A MEAN CUSS? ME! REALLY—!"

fun of flirtation on *your* side, and I wasn't afraid the emotional strain was going to shatter you up to any serious extent. Now it's left off amusing me, and I guess it's time to stop. I'm as perfectly aware as I can be that you've been searching around for some way of getting out of it this long while back—so there's no use of your denying you'll be real enchanted to get your liberty again!

CULCH. I may return your charming candour by admitting that my—er—dismissal will be—well, not wholly without its consolations.

MISS T. Then *that's* all right! And if you'll be obliging enough to hunt up my Poppa and send him along, I guess I can dispense with your further escort, and you can commence those consolations right away.

CULCH. (*alone*). The little vixen! Saw I was getting tired of it, and took care to strike first. Clever—but a trifle crude. But I'm free now. Unfortunately my freedom comes too late. Podbury's *Titania* is much too enamoured of those ass's ears of his—— How the brute will chuckle when he hears of this! But he won't hear of it from *me*. I'll go in and pack and be off to-morrow morning before he's up!

NEXT MORNING; IN THE HALL OF THE GRAND HOTEL DANDOLO.

THE GERMAN PORTER (*a stately person in a gold-laced uniform and a white waistcoat, escaping from importunate visitors*). In von momendt, Matam, I attend to you. You want a larcher roôm, Sare? You address ze manager, blease. Your dronks, Laties? I haf zem brod down, yes.

A LADY. Oh, Porter, we want a gondola this afternoon to go to the Lido, and *do* try if you can get us Beppo—that *nice* gondolier, you know, we had yesterday!

THE PORTER. Ach! I do nod know *any* nah-ice gondolier—zey are oal—I dell you, if you lif viz zem ade mons as me, you cot your troat—yes!

ANOTHER LADY. Porter, can you tell me the name of the song that man is singing in the barge there?

PORTER. I gannot dell you ze name—pecause zey sing always ze same ting!

A HELPLESS MAN IN KNICKERBOCKERS (*drifting in at the door*). Here, I say. We engaged rooms here by telegram from Florence.

The Pilgrims of Love. 139

What am I to give these fellows from the station? *Combien*, you know!

PORTER. You gif zem two franc—and zen zey vill gromble. You haf engage roôms? yes. Zat vill pe oal rahit—Your loggage in ze gondola, yes? I haf it taken op.

THE H. M. No, it's left behind at Bologna. My friend's gone back for it. And I say, think it will turn up all right?

PORTER. Eef you register it, and your vrient is zere, you ged it —yes.

THE H. M. Yes, but look *here*, don't you know? Oughtn't I to make a row—a fuss—about it, or something, eh?

PORTER (*moving off with subdued contempt*). Oh, you can make a foss, yes, if you like—you ged nossing!

CULCH. *and* PODB. (*stopping him simultaneously*). I say, I want my luggage brought down from No. — in time for the twelve o'clock— (*To each other.*) Hallo! are *you* off too?

CULCH. (*confused*). Er—yes—thought I might as well be getting back.

PODB. Then I—I suppose it's all settled—with Miss T.—you know —eh?

CULCH. Fortunately—yes. And—er—*your* engagement happily concluded?

PODB. Well, it's *concluded*, anyway. It's all *off*, you know. I—I wasn't artistic enough for her.

CULCH. She has refused you? My *dear* Podbury, I'm really delighted to hear this—at least, that is——

PODB. Oh, don't mind *me*. I'm getting over it. But I must congratulate you on better luck.

CULCH. On precisely similar luck. Miss Trotter and I—er—arrived at the conclusion last night that we were not formed to make each other's happiness.

PODB. Did you, by Jove? Porter, I say, never mind about that luggage. Do you happen to know if Mr. and Miss Trotter—the American gentleman and his daughter—are down yet?

The Travelling Companions.

PORTER. Trodders? Led me see, yes, zey ged zeir preakfast early, and start two hours since for Murano and Torcello.

PODB. Torcello? Why, that's where Bob and Miss Prendergast talked of going to-day! Culchard, old fellow, I've changed my mind. Shan't leave to-day, after all. I shall just nip over and see what sort of place Torcello is.

CULCH. Torcello—"the Mother of Venice!" it really seems a pity to go away without having seen it. Do you know, Podbury, I think I'll join you!

PODB. (*not over cordially*). Come along, then—only look sharp. Sure you don't mind? Miss Trotter will be there, you know!

CULCH. Exactly; and so—I think you said—will the—er—Prendergasts. (*To* PORTER.) Just get us a gondola and two rowers, will you, for Torcello. And tell them to row as fast as they can!

CHAPTER XXV.

Journeys End in Lovers' Meeting.

SCENE—*Near Torcello.* CULCHARD *and* PODBURY *are seated side by side in the gondola, which is threading its way between low banks, bright with clumps of Michaelmas daisies and pomegranate-trees laden with red fruit. Both* CULCHARD *and* PODBURY *are secretly nervous and anxious for encouragement.*

PODBURY (*humming* "*In Old Madrid*" *with sentiment*). La-doodle-um-La-doodle-oo : La-doodle-um-te-dumpty-loodle-oo ! I think she rather seemed to like me—those first days at Brussels, don't *you* ?

CULCHARD (*absently*). Did she? I dare say. (*Whistling* "*The Wedding March*" *softly.*) Few-fee; di-fee-fee-few-few; few-fiddledy-fee-fiddledy-few-few-few-fee. I fancy I'm right in my theory, eh?

PODB. Oh, I should say so—yes. *What* theory?

CULCH. (*annoyed*). What theory? Why, the one I've been explaining to you for the last ten minutes!—that all this harshness of hers lately is really, when you come to analyse it, a decidedly encouraging symptom.

PODB. But I shouldn't have said Miss Trotter was exactly *harsh* to me—lately, at all events.

CULCH. (*with impatience*). Miss Trotter! You! What an egoist you are, my dear fellow! I was referring to myself and Miss Prendergast. And you can't deny that, both at Nuremberg and Constance, she——

PODB. (*with careless optimism*). Oh, *she*'ll come round all right, never fear. I only wish I was half as safe with Miss Trotter!

CULCH. (*mollified*). Don't be too down-hearted, my dear Podbury.

I happen to know that she likes you—she told me as much last night. Did Miss Prendergast—er—say anything to that effect about *me?*

PODB. Well,—not exactly, old chap—not to me, at least. But I say, Miss Trotter didn't tell you *that?* Not *really?* Hooray! Then it's all right—she may have me after all!

CULCH. (*chillingly*). I should advise you not to be over-confident. (*A silence follows, which endures until they reach the landing-steps at Torcello.*) They *are* here, you see—those are evidently their gondolas, I recognise those two cloaks. Now the best thing *we* can do is to separate.

PODB. (*springing out*). Right you are! (*To himself.*) I'll draw the church first and see if she's there. (*Approaches the door of Santa Maria: a Voice within, apparently reading aloud:* " Six balls, or rather almonds, of purple marble veined with white are set around the edge of the pulpit, and form its only decoration.") Hypatia, by Jove! Narrow shave that!

[*He goes round to back.*

CULCH. (*comes up to the door*). I know I shall find her here. Lucky I know that Torcello chapter in "The Stones" very nearly by heart! (*Reaches threshold. A Voice within.* "*Well, I guess I'm going to climb up and sit in that old amphitheatre there, and see how it feels!*") Good heavens,—*Maud!* and I was as nearly as possible—I think I'll go up to the top of the Campanile and see if I can't discover where Hypatia is.

[*He ascends the tower.*

IN THE BELFRY.

PODB. (*arriving breathless, and finding* CULCHARD *craning eagerly forward*). Oh, so *you* came up too? Well, can you *see* her?

CULCH. Ssh! She's just turned the corner! (*Vexed.*) She's with Miss Trotter! . . . They're sitting down on the grass below!

PODB. Together? That's a nuisance! Now we shall have to wait till they separate—sure to squabble, sooner or later.

MISS T.'S VOICE (*which is perfectly audible above*). I guess we'll give Ruskin a rest now, Hypatia. I'm dying for a talk. I'm just as enchanted as I can be to hear you've dismissed Mr. Podbury. And I expect you can guess *why.*

Journeys End in Lovers' Meeting. 143

PODB. (*in a whisper*). I say, Culchard, they're going to talk about us. Ought we to listen, eh? Better let them know we're here?

"HYPATIA, BY JOVE! NARROW SHAVE THAT!"

CULCH. I really don't see any necessity—however,—(*Whistles feebly.*) Feedy-feedy-feedle!
 PODB. What is the use of fustling like that? (*Yödels.*) Lul-li-ety!
 MISS P.'S V. Well, my dear Maud, I confess that I——
 CULCH. It's quite impossible to make them hear down there, and it's

no fault of ours if their voices reach us occasionally. And it *does* seem to me, Podbury, that, in a matter which may be of vital importance to me—to us both—it would be absurd to be over-scrupulous. But of course you will please yourself. *I* intend to remain where I am.

[PODBURY *reluctantly resigns himself to the situation.*

MISS T.'S V. Now, Hypatia Prendergast, don't tell *me* you're not interested in him! And he's more real suited to you than ever Mr. Podbury was. Now, isn't that *so?*

CULCH. (*withdrawing his head*). Did you hear, Podbury? She's actually pleading for me! *Isn't* she an angel? Be quiet, now. I must hear the answer!

MISS P.'S V. I—I don't know, really. But, Maud, I want to speak to you about—Somebody. You can't think how he adores you, poor fellow! I have noticed it for a long time.

PODB. (*beaming*). Culchard! You heard? She's putting in a word for me. What a brick that girl is!

MISS T.'S V. I guess he's pretty good at concealing his feelings, then. He's been keeping far enough away!

MISS P.'S V. That was *my* fault. I *kept* him by me. You see, I believed you had quite decided to accept Mr. Culchard.

MISS T.'S V. Well, it does strike me that, considering he was adoring me all this time, he let himself be managed tolerable easy.

[PODBURY *shakes his head in protestation.*

MISS P.'S V. Ah, but let me explain. I could only keep him quiet by threatening to go home by myself, and dear Bob is such a devoted brother that——

PODB. Brother! I say, Culchard, she can't be meaning *Bob* all this time! She *can't!* can she now?

CULCH. How on earth can *I* tell? If it is so, you must be a philosopher, my dear fellow, and bear it—that's all.

MISS P.'S V. That *does* alter the case, doesn't it? And I may tell him there's some hope for him? You mustn't judge him by what he is with his friend, Mr. Podbury. Bob has such a *much* stronger and finer character!

MISS T.'S V. Oh well, if he couldn't stand up more on his edge than

Mr. Podbury! Not that I mind Mr. Podbury any, there's no harm in him, but he's too real frivolous to amount to much.

PODB. (*collapsing*). Frivolous! From *her* too! Oh, hang it *all!*
 [*He buries his head in his hands with a groan.*
MISS T.'S V. Well, see here, Hypatia. I'll take your brother on trial for a spell, to oblige you—there. I cann't say more at present. And now—about the other. I want to know just how you feel about him.

CULCH. The *other!*—that's Me! I wish to goodness you wouldn't make all that noise, Podbury, just when it's getting interesting!

MISS P.'S V. (*very low*). What is the good! Nothing will bring him back—*now!*

CULCH. Nothing? How little she knows me!

MISS T.'S V. I hope you don't consider *me* nothing. And a word from me would bring him along pretty smart. The only question is whether I'm to say it or not.

MISS T.'S V. (*muffled*). Dar-ling!

CULCH. I really think I might almost venture to go down now, eh, Podbury? (*No answer.*) Selfish brute! [*Indignantly.*

MISS T.'S V. But mind this—if he comes back, you've got to care for him the whole length of your boa—you won't persuade him to run in couples with anybody else. That's why he broke away the first time—and you were ever so mad with me because you thought I was at the bottom of it. But it was all his pride. He's too real independent to share chances with anybody alive.

CULCH. How thoroughly she understands me!

MISS T.'S V. And I guess Charley will grow out of the great Amurrcan Novel in time—it's not going ever to grow out of *him*, anyway!

CULCH. (*bewildered*). Charley? I don't see why she should mention Van Boodeler *now!*

MISS T.'S V. I like Charley ever so much, and I'm not going to have him cavort around along with a circus of suitors under vows. So, if I thought there was any chance of—well, say Mr. Culchard——

MISS P.'S V. (*indignant*). Maud! how *can* you? That odious hypocritical creature! If you knew how I despised and—— !

Miss T.'s V. Well, my dear, he's pretty paltry—but we'll let him go at that—I guess his shares have gone down considerable all round.

Culch. Podbury, I—I—this conversation is evidently not intended for—for other ears—I don't know whether *you* have heard enough, *I* shall go down!

Podb. (*with a ghastly chuckle*). Like your shares, eh, old chap? And mine too, for that matter. Well, *I'm* ready enough to go. Only, for goodness' sake, let's get away without being seen!

[*They slip softly down the series of inclined planes, and out to the steps, where they re-embark. As their gondola pushes off,* Mr. Trotter *and* Bob Prendergast *appear from the Museum.*

Mr. T. Why, land sakes! ain't that Mr. Podbury and Mr. Culchard? Hi! you ain't ever going away? There's my darter and Miss Hypatia around somewhere—They'll be dreadful disappointed to have missed you!

Podb. (*with an heroic attempt at cheeriness*). We—we're awfully disappointed to have missed *them*, Mr. Trotter. Afraid we can't stop now! Good-bye!

[Culchard *pulls his hat-brim over his eyes and makes a sign to the gondoliers to get on quickly;* Mr. Trotter *comments with audible astonishment on their departure to* Bob, *who preserves a discreet silence.*

CHAPTER XXVI.

Podbury kisses the Rod.

SCENE—*On the Lagoons.* CULCHARD *and* PODBURY'S *gondola is nearing Venice. The apricot-tinted diaper on the façade of the Ducal Palace is already distinguishable, and behind its battlements the pearl-grey domes of St. Mark's shimmer in the warm air.* CULCHARD *and* PODBURY *have hardly exchanged a sentence as yet. The former has just left off lugubriously whistling as much as he can remember of* "*Che faro*," *the latter is still humming* "*The Dead March in Saul*," *although in a livelier manner than at first.*

CULCH. Well, my dear Podbury, our—er—expedition has turned out rather disastrously!

PODB. (*suspending the "Dead March," chokily*). Not much mistake about *that*—but there, it's no good talking about it. Jolly that brown and yellow sail looks on the fruit barge there. See?

CULCH. (*sardonically*). Isn't it a little late in the day to be cultivating an eye for colour? I was about to say that those two girls have treated us infamously. I say deliberately, my dear Podbury, *infamously!*

PODB. Now drop it, Culchard, do you hear? I won't hear a word against either of them. It serves us jolly well right for not knowing our own minds better—though I no more dreamed that old Bob would ——Oh, hang it, I can't talk about it yet!

CULCH. That's childishness, my dear fellow; you *ought* to talk about it—it will do you good. And really, I'm not at all sure, after all, that we have not both of us had a fortunate escape. One is very apt to—er—overrate the fascinations of persons one meets abroad. Now neither of those two was *quite*——

PODB. (*desperately*). Take care! I swear I'll pitch you out of this gondola, unless you stop that jabber!

CULCH. (*with wounded dignity*). I am willing to make allowance for your state of mind, Podbury, but such an expression as—as *jabber*, applied to my—er—well-meant attempts at consolation, and just as I was about to propose an arrangement—really, it's *too* much! The moment we reach the hotel, I will relieve you from any further infliction from (*bitterly*) what you are pleased to call my "jabber"!

PODB. (*sulkily*). Very well—I'm sure *I* don't care! (*To himself.*) Even old Culchard won't have anything to do with me now! I must have *somebody* to talk to—or I shall go off my head! (*Aloud.*) I say, old *chap!* (*No answer.*) Look here—it's bad enough as it is without *our* having a row! Never mind anything I said.

CULCH. I *do* mind—I *must*. I am not accustomed to hear myself called a—a *jabberer!*

PODB. I *didn't* call you a jabberer—I only said you *talked* jabber. I—I hardly know what I *do* say, when I'm like this. And I'm deuced sorry I spoke—there!

CULCH. (*relaxing*). Well, do you withdraw jabber?

PODB. Certainly, old chap. I *like* you to talk, only not—not against Her, you know! What were you going to propose?

CULCH. Well, my idea was this. My leave is practically unlimited—at least, without vanity, I think I may say that my Chief sufficiently appreciates my services not to make a fuss about a few extra days. So I thought I'd just run down to Florence and Naples, and perhaps catch a P. & O. at Brindisi. I suppose *you're* not tied to time in any way?

PODB. (*dolefully*). Free as a bird! If the Governor had wanted me back in the City, he'd have let me know it. Well?

CULCH. Well, if you like to come with me, I—I shall be very pleased to have your company.

PODB. (*considering*). I don't care if I do—it may cheer me up a bit. Florence, eh?—and Naples? I shouldn't mind a look at Florence. Or Rome. How about Rome, now?

Podbury kisses the Rod.

CULCH. (*to himself*). Was I wise to expose myself to this sort of thing *again*? I'm almost sorry I——(*Aloud.*) My dear fellow, if we are to travel together in any sort of comfort, you must leave all details to *me*. And there's one thing I *do* insist on. In future we must keep to our original resolution—not to be drawn into any chance acquaintanceship. I don't want to reproach you, but if, when we were first at Brussels, you had not allowed yourself to get so intimate with the Trotters all this would never——

PODB. (*exasperated*). There you go again! I can't stand being jawed at, Culchard, and I won't!

CULCH. I am no more conscious of "jawing" than "jabbering," and if *that* is how I am to be spoken to——!

PODB. I know. Look here, it's no use. You must go to Florence by yourself. I simply don't feel up to it, and that's the truth. I shall just potter about here till—till *they* go.

CULCH. As you choose. I gave you the opportunity—out of kindness. If you prefer to make yourself ridiculous by hanging about here, it's no concern of mine. I dare say I shall enjoy Florence at least as well by myself.

[*He sulks until they arrive at the Hotel Dandolo, where they are received on the steps by the* PORTER.

PORTER. Goot afternoon, Schendlemen. You have a bleasant dimes at Torcello, yes? Ach! you haf gif your gondoliers vifdeen franc? Zey schwindle you, oal ze gondoliers alvays schwindles eferypody, yes! Zere is som ledders for you. I vetch them. [*He bustles away.*

MR. BELLERBY (*suddenly emerging from a recess in the entrance, as he recognises* CULCHARD). Why, bless me, there's a face I know! Met at Lugano, didn't we? To be sure—very pleasant chat we had too! So you're at Venice, eh? I know every stone of it by heart, as I needn't say. The first time I was ever at Venice——

CULCH. (*taking a bulky envelope from the* PORTER). Just so—how are you? Er—will you excuse me?

[*He opens the envelope, and finds a blue official-looking enclosure, which he reads with a gradually lengthening countenance.*

150 *The Travelling Companions.*

Mr. B. (*as* Culchard *thrusts the letter angrily in his pocket*). You're new to Venice, I think? Well, just let me give you a word of advice.

READS WITH A GRADUALLY LENGTHENING COUNTENANCE.

Now you *are* here—you make them give you some tunny. Insist on it, Sir. Why, when I was here first——

Culch. (*impatiently*). I know. I mean, you told me that before. And I *have* tasted tunny.

Podbury kisses the Rod.

Mr. B. Ha! well, what did you think of it? *Delicious*, eh?
Culch. (*forgetting all his manners*). Beastly, Sir, *beastly!*
  [*Leaves the scandalized* Mr. B. *abruptly, and rushes off to get a telegram form at the bureau.*
  Mr. Crawley Strutt (*pouncing on* Podbury *in the hall, as he finishes the perusal of his letter*). Excuse me—but surely I have the honour of addressing Lord George Gumbleton? You may perhaps just recollect, my Lord——?
  Podb. (*blankly*). Think you've made a mistake, really.
  Mr. C. S. Is it possible! I have come across so many people while I've been away that—but surely we have met *somewhere*? Why, of course, Sir John Jubber! you must pardon me, Sir John——
  Podb. (*recognizing him*). My name's Podbury—plain Podbury, but you're quite right. You *have* met me—and you've met my bootmaker too, "Lord Uppersole," eh? That's where the mistake came in!
  Mr. C. S. (*with hauteur*). I think not, Sir; I have no recollection of the circumstance. I see now your face is quite unfamiliar to me.
  [*He moves away;* Podbury *gets a telegram form and sits down at a table in the hall opposite* Culchard.
  Culch. (*reading over his telegram*). "Yours just received. Am returning immediately."
  Podb. (*do., do.*). "Letter to hand. No end sorry. Start at once." (*Seeing* Culchard.) Writing to Florence for room, eh?
  Culch. Er—no. The fact is, I've just heard from my Chief—a— a most intemperate communication, insisting on my instant return to my duties! I shall have to humour him, I suppose, and leave at once.
  Podb. So shall I. No end of a shirty letter from the Governor. Wants to know how much longer I expect him to be tied to the office. Old humbug, when he only turns up twice a week for a couple of hours!
  The Porter. Beg your bardons, Schendlemen, but if you haf qvide done vid ze schtamps on your ledders, I gollect bostage-schtamps, yes.
  Culch. (*irritably flings him the envelope*). Oh, confound it all, take

them. *I* don't want them! (*He looks at his letter once more.*) I say, Podbury, it—it's worse than I thought. This thing's a week old! Must have been lying in my rooms all this time—or else in that infernal Italian post!

PODB. Whew, old chap! I say, I wouldn't be *you* for something! Won't you catch it when you *do* turn up? But look here—as things are, we may as well travel *home* together, eh?

CULCH. (*with a flicker of resentment*). In spite of my tendency to "jaw" and "jabber"?

PODB. Oh, never mind all that now. We're companions in misfortune, you know, and we'd better stick together, and keep each other's spirits up. After all, you're in a much worse hat than *I* am!

CULCH. If *that's* the way you propose to keep my spirits up!—— But let us keep together, by all means, if you wish it, and just go and find out when the next train starts, will you? (*To himself, as* PODBURY *departs*.) I must put up with him a little longer, I suppose. Ah me! *How* differently I should be feeling now, if Hypatia had only been true to herself. But that's all over, and I dare say it's better so . . . I dare say!

[*He strolls into the hotel garden, and begins to read his Chief's missives once more, in the hope of deciphering some faint encouragement between the lines.*

FINIS.

Richard Clay & Sons, Limited, London & Bungay.

www.ingramcontent.com/pod-product-compliance
Lightning Source LLC
Chambersburg PA
CBHW030318170426
43202CB00009B/1056